THE CHRISTIAN INVESTOR
BE YOUR OWN BANK

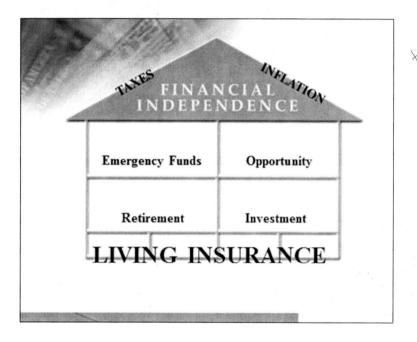

THE SECRET TO TAX-FREE WEALTH CREATION

PROSPER ENONGENE

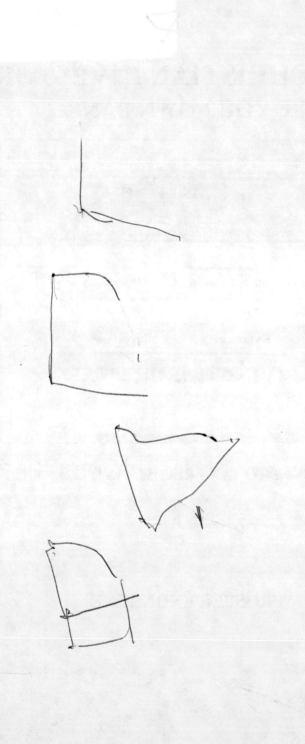

THE CHRISTIAN INVESTOR

Be Your Own Bank

THE SECRET TO TAX-FREE WEALTH CREATION

Prosper Enongene

The Christian Investor
Be your own bank
by Prosper Enongene

Printed in the United States of America

ISBN 9781613792568

Edited by: Mrs.Normell Guyden
            Sis. Bola Aibinuomo

You can contact the author at:
Phone: 713 576 9026 or 832 404 7837
Email:pros4jesus@yahoo.com

www.xulonpress.com

Dedication

This book is dedicated to Jehovah El-shaddai, the God who gave me the inspiration to write this. Thank you Lord for giving us the power to create wealth.
I also dedicate this book to my beautiful wife, Pastor Mrs. Cidoline Enongene. You are the honey sweet to my taste.
To my son, Immanuel Josia Prosper, may you become a kingdom financier.
And to all those who are ready for wealth transfer intended for the kingdom business.

Acknowledgements

My sincere thanks goes to Pastors John and Bridget Israel for their continual support and encouragement for this message to reach the body of Christ.

To Mrs.Normell Guyden, for using her editor's eye to pick out every mistake. Your work was awesome;

To Dr. Allison Wiley and Sis.Bola Aibinuomo for proof-reading this material.

Many thanks to Sis.Terra Jones for the graphic design work.

To all those who endorsed this material; your comments were so encouraging.

To all business partners who spent time reading the manuscripts; your suggestions were worthwhile.

Lastly, a vote of thanks to all those who encouraged me during this project especially my Zion family. You are the best.

What others are saying about the Christian Investor.....

"**M**y people are destroyed for lack of knowledge"(Hosea 4:6).It is said that 3% of the world's population own as much as the other 97%.You may be wondering why this is so. Simply put, 97% of the world population has been socialized to work only for money instead of allowing money working for them. The author, Prosper Enongene for the "Christian Investor" has provided valuable information to the Christian community as well as the non-Christian community to enable us to break the trend of systematic poverty and to usher us into a new realm of divine prosperity."

DR. Honorable Phillip S Phinn (OIA)
Order of International Ambassadors
Author of <u>Seven (7) Keys to Economic Empowerment</u>
And <u>How to Earn Multiple Income</u>
ITWLA Chief Ambassador to the United Nations.

As I look back on my theological training more than three years ago, much less attention was given to the secret of wealth creation than to biblical theology, doctrine and church history. Much damage has been done to the church and its member whereby people have questioned the power of God as a wealth creator and the rudiments for wealth creation. Case studies such as Isaac in the book of Genesis have not been expounded on fully for Christians to understand the need to invest faithfully in order to yield good returns. This is why this book is of such significance at a time that the world economy is facing challenges. Pastor Prosper, I perceived, has written out of his heart, knowing the debate that goes on within Christendom.

If anyone should be able to invest wisely and yield a hundred fold, I earnestly suggest this is a book to read. This book receives the seal of my blessings through Christ Jesus, who Himself was a valuable investment for reconciliation of man with His father.

Pastor Prosper has strived to keep out of the common by bringing to the fold a neglected topic. This is why his style of writing is simple but infectious as you navigate through its pages to encourage you to meditate on its various themes.

Reviewing this book is like visiting this topic for the very first time. There are many new concepts that are introduced which are of great significance if God's children are to make it in life and be in a pivotal position to support the kingdom. For those who are not too familiar with this terrain, it will be a breath of fresh air.

I learned from reading this book that God is the source and seed-giver. When we lean not on our own understanding and allow Him to provide, the spiritual fertilizers that we need our products will blossom beyond recognition. Despite the fact that Abraham was rich, it wasn't until he met with the owner of the source of wealth that he became rich.

It is also important that the author made mention of a moral duty that these men of God, including Abraham and Isaac, never neglected. Their wealth did not deter them from worshipping their God. They put Him first and recognized Him for all their financial achievement. As long as you partner with God in your investment, you will reap the reward that will make you enviable by those around you.

There is one infinite truth which is always neglected by God's children, but the author has articulated it accurately that; investing will help reduce the burden when the tide of life starts slowing down. He recommended that we should start building for the future at an earlier age. This, he suggested, might help us spend more time in kingdom business than "toiling all night and day with nothing to show for it." This is why he recommended that God should come first. There are many people in the kingdom who are working 24 hours a day traveling from one geographical location to another in view of becoming rich but have failed miserably without the "owner's" permission. It is indeed true, as the author pointed out, that having wealth will empower us to be sponsors in the kingdom and that role, in and of itself, will generate more wealth.

Being blessed with wealth has its own setbacks. Some of these, as he expressed, could be mismanagement of funds. There are businesses that have gone into liquidation due to mismanagement. There are also churches that have been closed due to accusations of embezzlement and misappropriation of funds.

We need to be financially comfortable as lack of it might lead to distress, hardship, and depression. Some people might suffer from ill health due to lack of amenities to sustain life.

The chapter on "Managing Life Insurances" is an eye opener for many who consider it a waste of time and waste of money. There are various terminologies and concepts within the Insurance discipline which one might not fully understand. This is why it is best to read this book and know the difference between life insurance and death or burial insurance to help you make a decision as to which one might be suitable.

Reviewing the chapter on "Stumbling Blocks and Barriers to Wealth Building" is the chapter to watch because most of us are guilty or responsible for our own failures. There is a saying in business psychology that "procrastination is an enemy to pragmatism". It simply means that we engage the mind thinking deeply of things to do but it is never accomplished. If we are to invest wisely and reap the benefits, we should take a step of faith and participate fully in investment for the future. The author expressed it frantically that to make a difference or to be fit for purpose, as an investor, we need to explore what is around for investment potential. We need to be financially disciplined if not the investment will go into liquidation.

In this world of information and exploration, one should not be ignorant about searching for the potential opportunities to invest. We need that knowledge to help locate the whereabouts of things to invest in. For us to boldly do that the fear syndrome should be abandoned. Fear will affect your decision to take a step of faith. God has not given you such characteristic but has given you sound mind so that you can think objectively and apply wisdom to aid your decision to invest.

I learned from reading and studying this book that the best insurance, however, is that which comes from God and that is the everlasting life insurance. Nevertheless, one should not be religious and fail to secure his/her life by opting out of any form of insurance schemes.

This author is very pragmatic in his approach. He made mention of a regular occurrence that has now become a regular feature with ministers of the gospel. Most of them are self-employed and could face financial difficulties if they are not wise enough to make investments and at the same time prepare for retirement. Ministers should be aware of investment possibilities instead of depending on love offerings. This is not reliable and cannot be solely depended upon. This is why the author inferred that there should be a paradigm shift in the way ministers preach the gospel. Issues of investment and preparing for the end of life should be part of teaching sessions which ministers should engage in with their members.

I do hope this book will find its way to the hands of many who are engaged in financial battles and looking for a way forward to invest wisely in his kingdom. I am sure it will be of benefit to the church and its proclamation of the gospel in the coming years. Pastor Prosper has meticulously disclosed and unleashed the most awesome revelations of how to create wealth and issues around insurance policies and end of life preparation. This has even enlivened me with an overwhelming and exciting expectancy dealing with my own life. Since reading this book, I have experienced a paradigm shift in life in the way I think of my finances. I have confidence that it will greatly impact your life as well.

Pastor (Dr) John Gbla Junior (International Evangelist, Teacher and Praise and Worship minister)
World Evangelism Bible Church (WEBIC).
London Headquarter Branch.
Ireland Dublin Branch Pastor.
Clinical Charge Nurse. (Healthy living Wellbeing Coordinator)
SHARP TEAM (Social Hope and Recovery Project).
South London and Maudsley NHS Foundation Trust. UK

I would greatly recommend this book to ministers; every member in my church will need to have a copy of this book.

Thank you, Pastor Prosper for revealing these secrets to the Body of Christ. I have never read a Christian book on this subject before in this manner. Your book is practical and it has changed my life.

The Christian Investor by Pastor Prosper Enongene provides much needed answers on how to manage money and make money work for you. Pastor Prosper bases his principles on the Bible and lives the principles that he writes about. Not only is Pastor Prosper an author, he is also the owner of The Way Multi-Services, a provider of investment services. He is a talented worship leader, songwriter, prayer warrior, a devoted pastor, husband and father. If you want to learn how to make money serve you, The Christian Investor is a definite must read.

Dr. Alison Wiley
President and Founder
Arise and Shining Enterprises, Inc. Houston TX

Wow, this is great. I wish I knew this long time ago.

Your book was an eye opener. I spent all night reading the manuscripts. I could not stop reading.

This is a well-written and informative book. As an Accountant and business woman I tell you what is written in this book will help you use and invest your money wisely. Let your money work for you not only you slaving for others. Money goes to those who do right with it. Wages will give you a living but investment will give you a fortune. As Christians, we need to follow the principles in the Bible about investing.

Regine Efeti Ojongtambia
MBA(Masters in Business Administration/Finance.
MPA (Masters in Public Accounting) Houston TX

A lot of us are slaves to the world's system because of lack of knowledge. Read this book. I HAVE MADE UP MY MIND TO BECOME A KINGDOM FINANCER. I love the way he uses scriptures to bring out the message of wealth creation. This book is practical, very informative and straightforward.

One of the chief disasters in Christian finances involves the failure to seek advice. In this book, God has anointed Pastor Prosper to be a blessing to believers and others by giving them a divine understanding and Godly counsel on how to better manage their wealth."

Bishop Kendall Baker, Senior Pastor,
Straight Up Ministries International Church,
Manager the 3-1-1 Service Center, Office of the Mayor, Houston Texas.

It is my great delight to endorse and recommend THE CHRISTIAN INVESTOR written by Minister Prosper Enongene. It is the prayer of the author that we prosper, increase and multiply. Please pay particular attention to the principles of paying yourself first, tax-free investment returns, protecting your seed and insurance protection. The book is right on time and target. We therefore pray and thank God for this precious man of God because Psalm 139: 6 says that "such knowledge is too wonderful for us".

Ifeanyi D. Onyekwena, Financial Consultant.
MBA,FCA,CIA,MCSE,CFE,CPA. Houston Tx

The <u>Christian Investor</u> is awesome because it touches on the key concepts of building Tax-Free wealth. The information outlined in the chapters of this book will enable financial planners and insurance agents help their clients build secured tax free wealth. I will encourage everyone in the financial business to read this book. It will change your life for good.

Dr Enongene Evaristus,
Etabang Enterprise Inc. Bowie MD

This book provides great information to change the financial situation of those who are ready for a change. My children will not be slaves to the system.

The "The Christian Investor" is an easy-read that brings to light the parallels of the character of a new testament Christian with that of any successful investor.

Derek Johnson (President) Capital Team financial
Beltsville, MD.

TABLE OF CONTENT

CHAPTER ONE

GOD BELIEVES IN INVESTMENTS

God is an investor. He believes in investments.

To invest basically means to sow a seed with an expectation of returns and profits. It is advisable to sow good seed in order to reap bountifully. The Webster dictionary says that it means *to furnish with power and authority, to endow with quality or characteristics, to commit (money) in order to earn a financial return, to expend for future benefits or advantages.*

Looking at the above definitions, the Lord God Almighty invested in us when He breathed into us the breath of life. At that moment, He released His characteristics, His attributes and His qualities into us. Then He blessed us and charged us to use His qualities in order to increase, to rule over and to multiply on earth. That means that God does not believe in stagnation. He invested His life into us as the seed for multiplication. He was and He is expecting bountiful returns and profits (Genesis 1:28 and 2:7). Read also Matthew 25:14-30.

He invested Jesus

"For God so loved the world that He gave His only begotten Son, that whoever believes in Him should not perish but have everlasting life" (John 3:16).

When the first investment failed, God turned around and invested His Son. Jesus, the lamb, was a sacrificial investment. Through His death and resurrection, we now have Christians all over the world. God's expectations for a profitable return were fulfilled. Jesus became the first born that led to many brethren (Romans 8:29). "For God so loved the world" that He invested Jesus, and Jesus so loved us that he gave His life (his all). He gave us the Holy Spirit, and the Holy Spirit so loved us that He decided to stay with us so that we could multiply with the anointing of the Holy Spirit (His power).

Jesus taught the principle of investing

"Most assuredly, I say to you, unless a grain of wheat falls into the ground and dies, it remains alone; but if it dies it produces much grain" (John 12:24).

Do something with the seed you have in order for increase and multiplication to kick in. Invest your seed into fertile grounds. You need to get or create a storehouse. You must leave your comfort zone (Matthew 13:3-8). The sower in this verse is the investor.

Righteous but Wealthy (Job of Uz)

You can still be righteous and wealthy. There is nothing like the saying, "poverty is next to godliness. That is actually a lie from the pit of hell. Poverty is instead, an enemy. Some often say that it is a disease. Others say that it is a curse. That is why the devil fights believers financially. He knows that if he brings you down financially, you will be unstable spiritually, ministry wise, and materially. Then he can strike from that very position. He wants to get us emotionally disturbed and physically worn out, and tired so that he can launch his attacks. You know very well that when you are broke, you become easily agitated. Any little biddy fly annoys you. Every phone call frightens you. You may be reading this book right now because you want to know the truth. Thank God for you. You are at the right place. Keep reading and you will know the truth that will eventually set you free.

The reason I brought this up is because of a man called Job. He was the greatest man of all in the east (Job1:2-3). But he was righteous and blameless (Job 1:1-8). He did not allow his wealth to get into his head. He maintained his sanity. So every good Christian investor should maintain a healthy relationship with the Lord after He has blessed and multiplied your seed.

THE FATHERS OF INVESTMENT (THE GREAT INVESTORS)

Abraham, Isaac, Jacob, David and Solomon and the present day Israelites applied principles of the Shepherd (their mentor) Jehovah –Rohi. He was their source. (John3:27). **God is the source and the seed giver.**

ABRAHAM (The Trader) (Genesis 12:1-2)

God was the one who blessed Abraham. He was the originator of Abraham's wealth. God will also use men to give you the seed. (Genesis 12:16) He will bless the seed and everything you touch. God did bless the seed and everything Abraham touched. Listen, when you are in God's divine plan and perfect will, whatever you touch will prosper. That is how Abraham became very rich, and richer and ultimately became the richest man in his days (Genesis 13:2, 24:1, 24:35). But to reach this level he did some trading. He traded in gold, silver and livestock. He even gave Lot, his nephew, seed to trade or invest. **Christian investors do help one another**. They became so big that the land could not contain them.

The way to the top involves sharing, team work and connectivity. They did not eat their seeds. Some of you right now have the seed but you are misusing it. Keep reading you will find help. They did not raise livestock just for themselves, but to leave a seed for the next generation.

Abraham set the pace that the next generation would follow. If you want to be a pacesetter for your family and generations to come; and if you are sick and tired of the misfortunes around you, don't worry, help is on the way. Abraham knew the power of un-ending streams of income, which is money coming from unlimited sources. With God being the blesser and the power behind his wealth, he created the path for generational wealth and passed it down to Isaac.

God does not have problems with us having great possessions as long as they do not take His place in our lives. Abraham was rich and loaded, but God called him his friend (2Chronicle20:7). God never complained about his wealth or him being carnal-minded. Having great possessions and living in abundance is in God's plan for His people (Genesis 15:14). God blessed him in all areas-financially, materially, and physically. The end was glorious (Genesis 24:1). **The end of a thing is better than the beginning**.

ISAAC (the investor) He followed divine leadership just like his father. He was not a squanderer. Even in a foreign land he prospered. So what is your own excuse, the excuse of being in full time ministry? Well, God told Isaac to invest and he became prosperous. Isaac was the kind of pastor that did not depend on a church offering or love offering because he was financially loaded. (Genesis 26:1-6, 12-14).

Vs. 12 "Then Isaac sowed in that land and reaped in the same year a hundredfold; and the Lord blessed him."

vs. 13 "The man began to prosper, and continued prospering until he became very prosperous;

vs. 14 for he had possessions of flocks and possessions of herds and a great number of servants. So the philistines envied him."

JACOB (The Entrepreneur) In Genesis 30:27-42, 43 He was able to take risks. Jacob became exceedingly prosperous not only because the hand of the Lord was upon him, but also he was determined to step out and start something for himself. **Christian investors should work to learn, they do not work just to earn**. They become independent so that God will send the blessing directly to them and not their employers (Laban). Be determined to go beyond raises and bonuses from your employers. Later on, as you keep reading, you will learn how to get rid of the Labans.

David and Solomon (The life insurance investors) 1Chronicles 22:1-14.

Before King David died, he made sure that he left behind everything his son needed to build the temple. In his own way, that was life insurance. Therefore Solomon did not ask God for material blessings because his father left behind everything he needed. He only needed the wisdom to manage the wealth that was passed to him. Some folks right now need just the wisdom to manage what they already have. You will find it. Keep reading. Solomon also, at the last stages of his life made a remarkable statement by the gift of wisdom which is being practiced today.

A good man leaves an inheritance to his children's children; But the wealth of the sinner is stored up for the righteous" (Proverbs 13:22).

CHAPTER TWO

BUILDING GENERATIONAL WEALTH

WHEN TO START

A year from now you will wish you had started today

The earlier the better, the younger the best. Parents should lock in their children as soon as they enter this world. Creating and building wealth starts when we are young so that when we get older our wealth will decrease our responsibilities. Remember the older we get the more responsibilities. How? Simple. When we are young we do not have a lot of financial needs as compared to adults. Therefore, we build and accumulate wealth because there are not many expenses on our part. There is little to worry about. For example, the responsibilities one has when twenty years young is not the kind that one will have when thirty. The younger, the best. This enables you to have enough time to enjoy your wealth when you really need it. you don't want to get so much wealth when you can't even eat a good steak or drive a Bentley. This can occur when you get too old. But you can't build wealth without protection.

Protection: Protection is the key to building wealth. If you don't have protection or security, the day you get sick, disabled, or if you die all that wealth will disappear into thin air. It baffles me how folks can protect their houses, cars, clothes, jewels, etc., but do not care to protect their money. They also dumped thousands of dollars into bank accounts and other investments portfolios and there is no protection on their money?

Now you may ask what kind of protection is he talking about? Well it's not FDIC. This is protection against your financial enemies. These enemies include lawsuits, taxation issues, recession, probates, liens, stock market (911). They can wipe out your wealth in a day. Therefore, try and get a life insurance investment such as life insurance that you don't have to die to use. It will give you the opportunity for tax free returns and the protection you need. If you die they pay, if you don't, you get back all your money with interest.

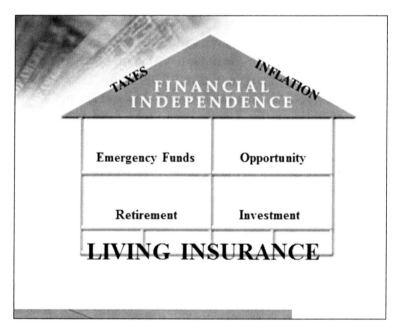

Living life insurance is the foundation to financial independence. It will protect your money from taxation and thereby reduces the effect of inflation on your money.

Why must you Invest? What's the purpose of money? Why does the Lord want us to be wealthy?

1) So that you can stop working 16/16:

Proverbs 23:4 Do not overwork to be rich; because of your own understanding, cease!

There are a lot of folks in this heartbreak. By the time they are five minutes into church services, they are fast at sleep. Most do not even show up for service anymore. May God help his people. The race is not for the swift. It is not how much you work. It is the Lord that will show you favor. That is why our prayer meetings and services are very powerless and boring because most of the folks are worn out. If members continue like this how and when are we going to fulfill the great commission? That's why God wants us to be wealthy so that we can work less and do more for the kingdom. He wants us to enjoy life. I have been there. I am just a spy from that land.

Proverbs 11:30 The fruit of the righteous is a tree of life, and he who wins a soul is wise.

2) To be a financial blessing to the church:

The church is not just a place for people to receive but also a place for us to give. She needs our finances to fulfill her mission on earth. If the people are broke how can they reach out to others? There are a lot of folks out there that need real financial assistance before they will see the four walls of a church. Our preaching alone will not do the job. Even Jesus had to feed the multitudes. Cry to God like Jabez did and your coast will be enlarged. Obey him as Paul did and the scales will fall off your eyes. The Lord knows where the money is. He will show you. He knows the fish or whatever/whosoever has the money.

3) It glorifies the Lord when we are wealthy:

Proverbs 19:7 All the brothers of the poor hate him; how much more do his friends go far from him! He may pursue them with words, yet they abandon him.

Folks do not pay much attention to broke people. We can't be representatives of El-shadai and we accept to be broke. We ought to be wealth distributors. The world needs to run to us for help. That is why I believe with all my heart, that any one that is determined to get financial freedom by seeking the face of the Lord, will overtake (Proverb 3:5-6). It is his will for us to be money-loaded so as to become wealth distributors. We can't go if we do not have the money. That is why most preachers are stuck within the four walls and they are not able to do much.

Proverbs 8:18, 21 Riches and honor are with me, enduring riches and righteousness. Verse 21, That I may cause those who love me to inherit wealth, that I may fill their treasuries.

4) Uncommon love for families: Love is also one of the fruits of the spirit. Galatians 5:22. If we do really love them we will plan for their tomorrow.

Proverbs 3:27 Do not withhold good from those to whom it is due, when it is in the power of your hand to do so.

1 timothy 5:8 But anyone who won't care for his own relatives when they need help, especially those living in his own family, has no right to say he is a Christian. Such a person is worse than the heathen (The living Bible).

5) For Charity work: There many hurting right now who need our help. But we will not be able to go and help around the world, if we do not have the financial freedom. Desire to be wealthy so that you can help orphans, widows and the less privileged.

6) For lean seasons: When you create a storehouse or have store-houses then you make yourself ready to supply to nations during famine, financial crisis, economic crisis, etc., (Genesis 41:56-57). That is how nations will come to your light when deep darkness covers the earth (Isaiah 60:1-3). They will come and borrow from Christian investors. Just like Joseph, the Lord has given to us all what it takes to excel in life. There are many of you praying for a financial blessing with no investment account. Let me ask you, where or into what is God going to pour out the blessing? You have been praying and fasting all your life, but add action to your prayer. **Faith without works is an excuse for laziness**.

7) So that you can **retire early and do God's work**: Numbers 8:24-25

'This is what pertains to the Levites: From twenty-five years old and above one may enter to perform service in the work of the taber-nacle of meeting; v.25, and at the age of fifty years they must cease performing this work, and shall work no more.

The day I saw this scripture my eyes popped out. Scales fell off my eyes. I was shocked because by God's standard at 50 we should at least officially retire, but a lot of folks at this age do not have any retirement plan. Not even the thought.

The 4 levels of income Earners

a) **Employees**: These are folks that live their lives from pay-check to paycheck. If they stop going to work for a few days their income also stops. Their bosses pay them just enough to keep them, so that they would not look for jobs some-where else. They are being paid just enough to come back next month. They receive just enough to pay their bills. Most of the people in this category are not being paid what they are really worth. This might not be you. But King Solomon called it an evil under the sun. Also most of the folks at this level do not have a lot of freedom, control or flexibility with their schedules. They take whatever offer is being made. Most can't go on vacation nor have free time for leisure at their own discretion.

A lot of folks at this level do not really like their jobs. They're just there because of the money. If you are doing something right now which is not your passion then you should get ready for boredom later on in life.

An employee simply means someone who depends on another person for their income. Child of God, listen, your employer can't pay you more than himself, and so you can't get any richer if you depend on his little bait. Wise up and think. Get rid of your Labans, like Jacob. The kingdom of God is at hand and the night cometh where no man will be able to work again. Stay with me and I will give you some clues of how to break out.

Investment options: This level consists of mostly 401(k), or 403(B) plans. These are the options most employers offer their employees. Again, just like the income, the employee does not have much control over these plans. That is why recently so many have lost so much money especially from their 401(K). Most of the contributors do not even know the 5 rules and restrictions that govern these plans. **This is not a good way to invest.**

b) **Self-employed**: These are independent contractors, brokers, consultants, and small business owners. They are their own bosses. They control their schedules or appointments. Most of them have the possibility to determine how much money they want to make. But some of them have difficulties with doing a lot of prospecting and marketing in order to make a sale. No sale, no income. Others have to open their doors of business and wait for clients or customers. If not they would not make money. Some of their **investment options include**: IRA,HR10, KEOGH PLANS. These plans are no good either because they are tax-deferred.

c) **Employer**: He has people working for him, but he still has to deal with chores of running a company. Though he has managers and administrative staffs, he still has to monitor the overall activities of the company. More often he has more worries than the employees. But this is a better place to be.

d) **Investor**: An investor is one who does not work for money but money is working for him. With a good vessel such as IUL, he or she doesn't have to worry about inventory, employees, and all the headaches that come with manage-ment. They do not have problems in leisure, such as playing golf, going on a cruise, and spreading the gospel. They relax, sit back and watch their money grow. You don't have to have a lot of money to be an investor. All you need is financial discipline. You need to learn to tell yourself, not to get what you don't need. An investor is who you should desire to be.

Now let me give you three rules of investment that will help you as a Christian investor.

Rule # 1- do not eat your seed. Proverbs 11:24
Rule # 2- never lose money
Rule # 3- don't break rule # 2

The retirement problem: Proverbs 15:13-14

1) **Lack of money:** It is a frightening thing to retire and you don't know how you going to spend the rest of your life without money. Statistics showed that majority of people who retired and went back to the job market was due to lack of finances. They took on more responsibilities like I said before. If the truth be spoken, most of these folks actually

prepared for retirement, but they used the wrong vessels or they were misinformed about the realities. You don't want to retire and find yourself at Wal-mart counting tickets, or scrubbing the floor at Jack in the box, or McDonalds.

You want to join your fellow retirees at the golf club or at the beach in Hawaii. We also found out that 53% of Americans are going to retire with less than $30.000. That is why folks need to know how to use tax-free investment vessels.

Proverbs 11:14 Where there is no counsel the people fall; but in the multitude of counselors there is safety.

2) **Motherland:** The idea to go back to the motherland will only work for those who are also investing in the motherland. Those who said they were going they are still here. They couldn't because the kids were still in school. They couldn't leave them with aunty Suzy, or Uncle Joe who might mess them up. So by the time the kids finished school they were already due for retirement.

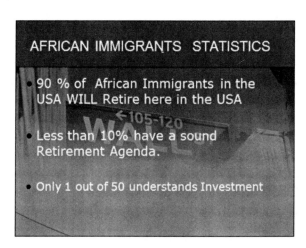

3) **Social security:** Most people might not get the social security they are anticipating to have when they retire. The reason being that most of the money is being used to finance wars.

Also, the present generation y is a computer age. They do not wish to work nor keep a job. Therefore social security will be affected because the present retirees are benefiting from those who are currently working. So by the time some of us retire there will be nothing left. As a matter of fact, this SSA (social security account) if changes are not enforced, will be exhausted by 2042. If you do not believe, go get your last statement and read what has been written on the right side of the front page.

4) **Relatives:** There are some people who have retired and they do not have a place to stay. These folks are squatting with friends or relatives. They did work all their life. But they ignored planning. That will not be your portion as you read this book.

5) **Go and Die:** No more strength. This is very true because the work force and corporate world has sapped every ounce of energy. Even doing the Lord's work is a problem. Please come out from amongst them.

Consequences of no investments

1) **Three jobs to live one life: (This is modern day slavery) "much ado about nothing."** Things fall apart. They're working hard with nothing to show. These are some of the complaints and statements from folks who never started early on to invest. When they were young they squandered all the money they had with unnecessary stuffs. Now that they are clocking 50, 55, 60, things are falling apart. They run from pillar to post, working three jobs to live one life, and they end up with nothing. The worst of all is that they end up with God's tithes in their pockets since they're trying to catch up. If this is you, keep reading, you do not need to work your life to death.

> *Proverb 23:4 Do not overwork to be rich; because of your own understanding, cease!*

2) **Family Embarrassments: Ecclesiastes 6:3-4** This is what the family gets if they had to beg to bury their love ones. This will not be your portion.

3) **Tithing: The house of worship will hardly see the 10% because money is tied.** Most churches have these kinds of folks. Therefore, there are huge crowds, but not enough to pay the bills. Pastors and ministers, if you want a financially healthy congregation, get your people financially educated. It will deliver you from chop-change collection, and it will move the vision forward. Remember the snake you avoid today might become the dragon before the day of your rest.

   Mismanagement of personal finance is one of the root causes of financial crisis. Most Believers experiencing financial crisis hardly pay tithes. A church that is healthy financially reaches out easily. This gospel is not only in words and there are some needs out there that will take more than prayer. I have been there, and I am still in the field. The financial needs out there are enormous. That is why some folks are retiring from evangelism. ANY CHURCH THAT IS NOT CREATING IMPACT IN THEIR COMMUNITY IS IRRELEVANT IN TODAYS SOCIETY.

4) **Absenteeism:** Pastors who complain about empty pews during services should keep on encouraging their folks to be financially independent. If they allowed their congregation to be educated in this area, they wouldn't worry about this roller coaster experience in church attendance. LATECOMING AND ABSENTEISM, (twin brothers), move from one generation to another. **Eighty per cent** of late coming and absenteeism is job related. Folks have to put in a lot of hours in order to meet up with the fast approaching retirement date lines. Therefore, they are forced to compromise God's time which results in lateness or they do not show up for services at all.

Hebrew 10:25 not forsaking the assembling of ourselves together, as is the manner of some, but exhorting one another, and so much the more as you see the day approaching.

5) **Spiritual Effect**: Most sheep with this crisis become spiritually weak and turn to remain weaker. Some even end up backsliding. What do you expect? What time do they have, reading the bible, praying and fellowshipping? Even when they do come to services they are not really interested in meat or the bone of the word. (Hebrew 6:1)All they want is milk.
6) **Depression:** leads to high blood pressure and other medical issues. Money crisis is always the number one stress factor. The effect of depression is devastating. It can kill when not well handled.
7) **Debts**: The scripture says a borrower is a slave to the lender. Folks with debts often get worried and stressed out because of frequent threats from the creditors. They can't sleep well.

> *Proverbs 22:7 The rich rule over the poor, and the borrower is servant to the lender.*

8) **Gambling** and **Cheating**: They would do things like these, not because they are bad Christians but because they are broke.

> *Proverbs 13:11 **states that** wealth from gambling quickly disappears; wealth from hard work grows (the living bible).*

Listen, I am not writing to belittle anybody. This is not the focus of this book, but it is to help some to see the dangers ahead so that they can think out of the box, take control over their finances, become good custodians of their money, and thereby become world changers.

Now let's take a look at life insurance investments.

CHAPTER THREE

MAJOR TYPES OF LIFE INSURANCE AND FEATURES

What you need to know before buying life insurance.

Term insurance: This is a temporary insurance. Coverage for the term of years that is specified in the contract. If the insured dies during this term, the policy pays the death benefits to the beneficiary. However, if the insured dies after the number of years specified in the contract, no death benefit is payable. For example, if you have 30 year term and you live for more than 30 years, no money will be given to your family. Term policies provide for the greatest amount of coverage for the lowest premium, as compared to any other form of protection. However, there is a maximum age which coverage will not be offered or renewed, such as 65 or 75.

Features and types of term insurance.

A) Convertible term: The policy contract can be converted to permanent coverage. But, the premium will be based on the insured's age at the time of conversion. Let's say you got a $100,000 policy at the age of 20 and you were paying $15 (per month). At the age of 50 you will have to pay an arm and a leg before conversion.

B) Renewable term: The policy owner can renew the coverage at the expiration date. Again the premium for the new term will be based on the insured's current age.
C) Level term: The premium is often level throughout the term of the policy. Death benefit might fluctuate.
D) Decreasing term: level premium with a death benefit that decreases each year.
E) Increasing term: level annual premium with a death benefits that increases each year over the duration of the policy term.

Return of premium: This is a rider or feature that is being attached to some of the term insurance in order for the insured to get back some of the premium paid at the end of the contract.

Permanent life insurance

1) Whole life: premiums and death benefits will remain level for life. Death benefit will never increase. Borrowed loans and interest must be paid back, if not it will be deducted from the face value at the insured's death. Examples of these kind of policy are limited pay life,-Lp85, Lp65, 7pay life, 20pay-life etc.
2) Universal life: known as flexible premium adjustable life. The death benefit can be increase or decrease depending on the insurance needs of the policy owner. It may pay itself if there is sufficient cash value in the policy. Under universal life we have fixed, variable and index universal life.

DEATH INSURANCE OR LIFE INSURANCE

The question that I will like to ask at this juncture is: do you have life or death insurance? Well, death insurance is the kind of policy which is meant specifically for burial. Most of them have limited pay periods-such as Lp85, Lp65, and Lp20 etc. Their face amount ranges from $1000 –$25,000. Most people I have met with the above product, have a death benefit which ranges between $7, 000 to $10,000. I don't know if this amount can still bury someone right now due to inflation. Any way when people die and leave these kinds of policies, their families do not have anything left after the burial. This is why I personally do not encourage folks to buy these kinds of policies. Most family instead sinks more into a deeper financial dungeon, especially if it was the bread winner that died. Proverb 13:22. A good man leaves an inheritance to his children's children, but the wealth of the sinners is stored up for the righteous.

The premiums of death insurance or the old kind of insurance are not flexible. If you miss one payment the policy falls into pending lapse. And if another premium is missed, that is the end of the policy. If you take money from the policy cash value, you have to pay it back, because you borrowed the money. If it is not paid back, the loan amount will be deducted from the insured's death benefit and the family may end up not having even enough to bury the insured. Some of you can relate to this either for yourself or for a loved one. Well keep on reading, your eyes will be opened.

The above kind of insurance is not the kind of insurance you can use to build up wealth. Life insurance really means insurance to help my life or other lives while I am alive. It means insurance for life expenses such as college expenses, sicknesses, retirement planning and other unforeseen life's events. Also at death, the policy's death benefit is capable of leaving generational wealth. This is the true meaning of life insurance. Some of us think that, if you buy life insurance you will not enjoy a penny out of it. No! This is a lie. Well, it depends on the kind of insurance we buy.

Folks who have been enlightened are taking advantage to build up wealth for themselves and their families. You see, the biggest devil standing between us and our breakthrough is ignorance. That is why this book was written, so that men and women of God can also know that there is a life insurance out there which they don't have to die to use, because it builds tax –free cash.

CHAPTER FOUR

BE YOUR OWN BANK

LIFE INSURANCE YOU DON'T HAVE TO DIE TO USE

Index universal life:

For those of you do not believe in life insurance you need to take a look at this product. It is a great investment vessel. This product brings out the real meaning of life insurance. Many have confused life insurance with death insurance.

Death insurance or burial insurance is not life insurance. The purpose as the name indicates is for burial. With this kind of insurance there are no living benefits. It is for funeral purposes and the balance to the beneficiaries, if there is any. You can't invest or save for retirement with burial insurance.

Index universal life features:

a) The premium-is flexible: The insured or the policy owner has the opportunity of controlling the premium as long as it is not below the minimum. **The owner** can increase or decrease the premium. You can even skip payments at tough times as long as there is enough cash value (money) inside the investment portfolio. This is a great feature because I know of people whose life insurance policy does not allow them to reduce payments or skip payments.

b) Death benefit or face amount: it has two options. Option A and option B.

Option A The death benefit remains level while the cash value (amount you can pull out of the policy before maturity) gradually increases.

Option B The death benefit increases each year by the amount that the cash value increases. At any point in time, the total death benefit will always be equal to the face amount of the policy plus the current amount of the cash value. Though the death benefit increases every year, the premium remains level. This helps the client not to bother about buying more insurance as he or she gets older.

c) *Un-employment benefits: As long as the client can prove that they are legally unemployed, the premium will be waived for 3months. All companies do not have this feature.*

d) *Interest rate- it is not fixed or variable: The floor is 1% or 2% (depending on which company), and the ceiling is 12%. Here you do not lose money like some other investment vessels out there. The money you invest is at 1 or 2% minimum and up to 12% **maximum**. You make money and maintain your money. When the market drops to minus you maintained the money you have accumulated and when it moves up, you move up.*

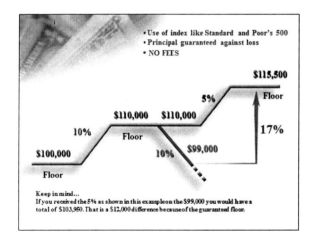

• Use of index like Standard and Poor's 500
• Principal guaranteed against loss
• NO FEES

$115,500
Floor
5%
$110,000 $110,000
10%
Floor
17%
$100,000
10% $99,000
Floor

Keep in mind...
If you received the 5% as shown in this example on the $99,000 you would have a total of $103,950. That is a $12,000 difference because of the guaranteed floor.

This is pretty good because it takes away the fear of loses in the market. It gives you peace and a good night sleep. You can plan for the future with your money with no surprises. If you have lost money through 401(K), mutual funds, stocks, CDS, and other vessels, then you need to consider this product.

Disability: This is a great rider because it helps you pay your bills and take care of your family while you are out of job. In most cases this is a paid rider and is not available with every company.

***Critical, chronic and terminal illnesses rider or living benefit —** are free with a company called lSW. You pay one single monthly pre-mium and get these riders plus an investment account, with a death benefit. This rider can be invoked while you're still alive. It pays you directly from your policy value while still alive if any of these conditions arises.*
Are you worried about your kid's college funds? Need money for a down payment for a house, for buying a new car? Are you worried about not having enough money for retirement and money for unforeseen emergencies? This product offers you the possi-bility of helping solve these problems.

Kid's college funds: most parents want to save or are saving right now for their kid's college tuition. But if they do not know the right vessel to use, most of the money will end up with the tax man or kids wouldn't have any financial aid. With IUL money accumulated is not counted as incometodetermine how much financial aid your children will receive as they gets ready to enter college. This is a very huge advantage. Proverbs 13:22, 1timothy 5:8

***IUL is a covered investment tool** Now let me differentiate between **covered** and **open investments**. A **Covered investment** is an investment whose account can't be accessed or frozen by your enemies. Nobody can put a lien on it. You have the money, but the cash is legally covered. No lawyer, loan officer, financial aid worker or prosecutor will be able to get access to that money. Not even your tax guy. The money is protected from creditors*

An Open investment, on the other hand, is exposed to unwanted visitors. Unwanted visitors are those who take advantage of others to make some money out of their money. Monies in bank accounts are vulnerable to these guys. Examples of such investment accounts includes saving accounts, money market accounts **CDs, checking accounts, properties, mutual funds, 403(b), 401(k), TSP etc.**

When friends tell me their accounts were frozen, or someone went in and got their money from their accounts; or they had a loss from the market, I know immediately that they do not know about covered investments. And don't forget that if someone files a law suit against you, your assets can be frozen. Your properties can be seized or a lien can be placed on them. The solution is to get a covered investment (life insurance you don't have to die to use). Below is a chart that shows you how the above mention items are being taxed.

TAX CLASSIFICATIONS ON PRODUCTS

TAX-FREE	TAX-NOW	TAX-LATER
Municipal Bonds	Bank CD, saving accounts, checking	IRA,401(K).403(B)
Roth IRA	Money market, stocks	Annuity(ies)TSP
Life insurance(with cash value)	Mutual funds	Pension plans
No tax on withdrawal	Tax each year	Tax on withdrawal.

Rule of 72 *(power of compound interest)*
Deuteronomy 8:13(The Anointing of Multiplication)
How it works:

A		B		C	
72/4=18 Money doubles every 18 years		Money doubles every 9 months		Money doubles every 6 years	
Age	4%	Age	8%	Age	12%
29	10,000	29	10,000	29	10,000
47	20,000	38	20,000	35	20,000
65	40,000	47	40,000	41	40,000
		56	80,000	47	80,000
		65	160,000	53	160,000
				59	320,000
				65	640,000

The rule of 72 can help you to determine how long it will take your money to double in any investment or savings. Simply divide 72 by the interest rate. In this illustration, Investor A's money will double every 18 years. B's money will double every 9 years and C's money will double every 6 years. That is why it is very important to know where to save or invest. Interest rates plays a great role in determining how much money you will accumulate in your port-folio. In the above illustration Investor C is in a better position than the others. That is why it is not how much you work hard, but how you get yourself informed and educated with the right information from the right source. For most people investing or saving for col-lege or retirement is not the problem, but how to and where to invest is the problem.

Let's assume Investor A went to one of the banks at the corner of the street and opened a 4% CD account. At the age of 65 when he retires his $40,000 will be affected by taxation. He will have to pay his taxes based on the % of the tax bracket at the time, not when he deposited his 10,000 at the bank. Also inflation will make the remaining cash valueless. In addition to that, because his CD account was not a covered investment, his CD account will be a deciding factor towards the amount of financial aid his kids will receive. Let's also assume Investor C invested through IUL. His money will be covered. It will grow tax-free and he will also receive his money tax-free.

However, the performance of investment fluctuates, so the actual time it takes an investment to double, cannot not be predicted with any certainty. And there is no guarantee that an investment or savings account can outpace inflation. All figures in the above chart are for illustrative purposes only… **to increase your financial IQ, protect your money tax-free.**

Saving Account

The story of Miss Bologna Njin.

*Miss Bologna works at the bank. She came to know the IUL product through one of her customer's. The client went to the bank and told Miss Njin that she wanted to close her saving account. When Miss Njin asked her why, she said she found a product that will give her a better return on her investment. The client whose name can't be mention right now has been saving for retirement through her saving account. By this time her account was having $30.000. But the problem was, this amount was simply her principal. Only a few dollars had been added to it since she started. She got frustrated with no growth. Remember the rule of 72 with this account's interest rate which we were not told, might take 30 years for the money to double. So on this faithful day she decided to withdraw the money. But as Miss Njin insisted on her maintaining the account, she screamed, No! I need my money. I have found a man who has shown me a better way. The bank teller (Miss Njin) asked "where is the man?" The client beckoned to my friend who was sitting at the lobby. Miss Njin called my good old friend. My friend shared with her the little secret behind **IUL** and she decided to set up an appointment for herself and her husband. After the presentation, the husband of Miss Njin did not only sign up for IUL but decided to become an advocate of the good news, by helping others.*

The purpose of this story is to let you know that knowledge is **power.** *It is not how much we work, but how much good* **information** *you receive that will change our situation. If we keep on doing the same thing every day, we will keep on having the same results. Thus we remain the same.*

Folks who live from pay check to paycheck, and put their money in one bogus account, which they do not know all the rules and restrictions, will never retire. Most often they retire broke. Get wisdom, get understanding. Saving accounts are not for investments purposes. There are for certain emergencies and for the banks to make money off your money through credit card business and loans. There are to saved money, for delayed spending. The lady in this story had to pull out all her money because she was just working for the bank. Banks are not your friends when it comes to investments. Watch out.

There is a difference between saving money and investing money. Saving money is like keeping your furniture in storage, and investing money is like planting a seed in a ground for growth and multiplication. Saving money is short term, while investing money is long term. Saving money increases your money whereas investing money multiples your money. A saver is limited. An investor is limitless.

IUL AND 401(k)/IRA

If you have a 401(k), I want you to know that, it is not your employer that is investing the money you contribute. Your company has an investor. It might be a bank or a financial service company that invests that money for you. You need to know the investor before you quit that job or go somewhere else. Keep all the paper work for references and follow ups. I brought this up because recently I ran into a lady who told me that she could not track down her 401(k) because her company had folded up. This problem occurred as a result of negligence. When her company folded up, a couple years ago, she was not really concerned about her 401(k). She had misplaced all the paper work; and when her eyes were opened years afterwards, she became frustrated. Be a good custodian of your money. Don't work for others. Track down the money you are working for. Some folks have been going for days without sleep looking for those slips. Therefore, make good use out of it. The chart below will give a clear distinction between IUL and 401(k).

IUL	*401(k)*
Has protection in case of death	*No protection*
Is a covered investment	*Open investment*
Gains are tax-free	*Gains are taxed. Will be taxed at your current tax bracket.*
You can have your money with no penalties during emergencies	*10% penalties*
No loss to your gains	*You can suffer losses*
You are in full control	*Partial control*
Have protection against critical, chronic and terminal illnesses-free *Money grows consecutively*	No living benefits Hidden fees, limited amount to contribute, Must get all contributions out at age 701/2 Aggressive, but risky
Long term investment-after 10 years	Long term investment after 59 ½ years

Individual situation might vary. This is just for illustration purposes.

I would like to emphasize that if the gains of the IUL are well structured **you pay no income tax ever.** *Whereas in the typical straight pension plans, like those open investment products listed above, you pay taxes on the gains and they are loaded with hidden* *charges and fees. Some of you do not even care to read your annual statements from your pension plans. I want to challenge you to call your money managers and ask them to explain all the fees on your statement. You will be shocked to find out that they do not have the plan they call pension plan for their own pension.*

THE POWER OF THE LSW-IUL LIVING BENEFITS

The story of Miss Brown: Miss Brown, sweet grand ma, was attacked with cancer. The doctor told her she needed $200.000 to go through a major surgery. She did not have that kind of money. But she decided to call her **LWS-IUL** *company to find out if they could help. Well they told her she had a death benefit of $600,000 and based on her contract, the living benefit option would be able to give her at least $200,000. But they told her that the withdrawn amount would reduce her death benefit to $400,000. Off course she said no problem because that was exactly what she needed. She took the money, cured herself and today she has her life back.*

This is what will call life insurance. You don't have to die to use it. Why must you have to die before the insurance company will now release $600,000 to your family? You might say but she was an old woman. You're right. What if it was a young bread winner of a family? And we see this happening to key members of families every now and then. Get wisdom, get understanding and get the right kind of insurance. It will save a life and save your money from Uncle Sam.

What does life insurance you don't have to die means?

It means: **access to your policy's death benefit while you are still living.** *I repeat while you are still alive. How many persons do you know that had cancer, stroke, heart attack, organ transplant, kidney failure, multiplesclorosis or any critical, chronic or terminal illness but ended up dying even though they had some kind of life insurance?. The reason is mostly because the doctors could not continue the treatment because there was no money. We all know that the purpose of the death benefit is for the beneficiary after the death of* *the insured. But in this case if an insured is attacked with a terminal, chronic or critical illness they can access a particular % of their death benefit with this product. Life events such as these can happen at any time and most often without warning.*

Example2: A husband and father of two suffered a severe heart attack at the age of 54. There was no other source of income for this guy. But fortunately for him he had a death benefit of 250,000 with this product. He was able to use his critical illness rider to access up to 150,000 from his death benefit of 250.000. He used the cash to pay his medical bills and the balance was used to pay off his house. This is the real meaning of life insurance. It is different from burial insurance. Helping families when they need the money the most and rescuing a life from dying is what we call life insurance. That means it is designed to take care of you while you are still alive. This is not the death insurance which some folks call life insurance. Some end up not buying life insurance because they think that they are going to die very soon. No! Real life insurance helps you to invest for the future.

With this product, you also have access to your accumulated investment for events such as education, a down payment for a house, retirement income or whatever you want to do with your money. And remember you don't really have to pay back this money. It also means private equity banking.

PRIVATE EQUITY BANKING

Fewer than 5 % of retired Americans have income over 3k per month. Even with a 401(k) or IRA, or other tax-deferred vehicles, it is not likely that you are saving enough for retirement, because tax-deferred still means taxes and upon retirement you may even pay more taxes because of fewer deductions. For example, by the time most folks retire they have fewer or no more kids in college and no more mortgages. Therefore, by the time most people retire they will realize that there is very little or absolutely nothing in their retire-ment saving plans because of taxes and inflation.

Now assume a scenario where you get paid $100 and your tax bracket is 30% like most of us. Your take home pay is about $70. Now 95% of the things you buy (gasoline, basic home items, Starbuck coffee, chewing gum, clothes, etc.) with that $70 will cost you another 35% of taxes, which means your actual take home pay is about $35. This is the exact amount you will have to pay mortgage/rents, car loans and other bills. What that tells you is that the government gets you at the front end and also at the back end. But the good news is that many government regulations have grandfather clauses, carefully buried in the tax codes.

So what is the solution?

Section 7702 of the tax code allows legal reserve insurance companies to construct **long term cash accumulated life insurance contracts that do not require any taxation on the growth of your money**. *It is not tax deferred like 401k, 403b, TSp, IRA. It is tax exempt like the money you can get out of your home equity tax free. But the advantage with this over home equity is that, there is no income qualification, credit check, and your rent does not go up. Major banks like Bank of America, Wells Fargo, Wachovia and Citti Group does contribute over 13 billion, 12 billion,3 billion, respectively into 7702. It is a major part of their asset allocation over real estate. Why? Taxes, Taxes, Taxes!!!!!!!*

These **insurance contracts** *do not allow you to deposit your money without taxation, but they do compound your interest earnings without taxation, and they do pay out your retirement income without taxation. The limit of how much you can put is based on your total insurance value.* **You can put millions into it in one year which you can't do with regular pension plans**. *Furthermore, your interest earnings are based on a balanced and diversified market indexed of publicly traded securities like the S&P 500, the Dow Jones and the NASDAQ, but without actually buying/selling any stock. Moreover, there are no allocations because the indexed is already balanced and diversified. Unlike the tax deferred accounts, there are* **no hidden fees**. *It has inbuilt guarantee/protection with* living benefits and limited risk of loss. Because, when the index is positive you gain and when the index is negative you stay where you are. Of course, you do not get all the gain, but you do not also get any of the loss. Once you earn it, you keep it. In addition several of these policies (contracts) have inbuilt living **benefits,** which in case of a serious injury or sicknesses, one can invoke to use the face value as a source of emergency funding.

How does 7702 enable one to open a bank?

First set up a life insurance contract with a reputable company. Let me also say that there is no insurance that is a gold standard. Every product is designed for a target market, so if someone tells you their product is the best, then they are lying to you. A good agent or broker should be able to outline to you the differences in products and show you all the riders you can qualify for. Rule of thumb, whenever insurance is cheap, just know that you have limited benefits and do not forget that the states allow the companies a two year contestability option. That is why cancelling some type of policies in the early year may be harmful. One thing you should be cautious about is listening to uncles and aunties or anyone who are not credible license holders, and **who do not have sound knowledge** of the product portfolios. You may be investing penny wise and pound foolish because you want to please uncle Deno.

Secondly, you need to capitalize your bank by paying your premium. It could be a onetime dump(single) since 7702 allows over funding of your policy up to the MEC limit. This is usually the fastest way to raise your venture capital, if you have the money. Others do monthly or annual funding depending on their individual needs and wants. But you need to consult with a professional to guide you on this journey so that you stay within your budget or else you may lapse the policy and that is not good news, especially during the first years.

Why now?

You might be saying, if this is true how come I have not heard about it. No!! You heard about it but you did not know how to use it to your advantage. This an old commodity that several universities endowment programs, large corporations and banks have used for decades to provide a safe long term bet as well as provide high rates of returns to fund employee and retirees benefits. It is very competitive to CD, money market and 401ks, but has the dramatic advantage in that you pay no income tax ever on the gains, if the insurance contracts are structured properly and the withdrawals are done based on the tax laws.

Examples:

In today's volatile and less secured market with money market at 2% and 5yrs CD at 3%, the annual rate of return on these products is within 4-8%, and has the tax exempt advantages over tax-deferred accounts. In the 1930's JC Penny used cash value insurance for payroll during the great depression. In 1953, Walt Disney took advantage of private equity banking, (cash value insurance), to build Disney world in Orlando, Florida. Since 2006, I have opened three separate personal accounts. The annual rate of returns on these has never fallen below 5% even with economic depression of 2008. Even with the AIG debacle, which was not really a true issue, the general insurance industry is still double AA rating. That's why 50 banks failed in 2009/2010, but not a single insurance company failed. At the moment 860 banks are on the trouble list. Why, because in reality banks are just gate keepers for insurance companies, who are the true controllers of the money you deposit. You see insurance companies are legal reserve entities, unlike banks where your FDIC insure amount is 250k. But insurance companies are required by law to maintain capital reserves (in billions) for all their contractual agreements. Now let me ask you, have you ever thought for a second where most rich folks keep their millions of dollars? Now you know. They use capital reserves companies. Insurance contracts unlike banks are protected from probate law suits. Its cash value is not considered an asset for Kids College financial indexed calculations. That is why it beats the favorite ROTH IRA, Municipal bonds, and 529 college plans.

Policy Year	Age	Annual Outlay	Guaranteed Cash Value	Guaranteed Death Benefit	Current Cash Value	Current Death Benefit	Annual Income
		7,800	3,913	381,573	4,077	381,737	0
		7,800	9,019	388,179	9,682	388,843	0
		7,800	16,191	394,897	17,723	396,429	0
		7,800	23,473	401,730	26,277	404,533	0
		7,800	30,473	408,682	35,391	413,193	0
		7,800	38,879	415,544	45,101	422,450	0
		7,800	45622	422,517	55,451	432,345	0
		7,800	53,166	429,607	66,476	442,917	0
		7,800	60,829	436,819	78,226	454,217	0
		7,800	68,617	444,154	91,844	467,381	0
		78,000					0
		7,800	76,525	451,608	107,127	482,210	0
		7,800	84,098	459,181	123,182	498,265	0
		7,800	91,789	466,872	14,547	515,630	0
		7,800	99,592	474,675	159,304	534,387	0
		7,800	107,501	482,584	179,588	554,671	0
		7,800	115,513	490,596	201,536	576,619	0
		7,800	123,616	498,699	225,277	600,360	0
		7,800	131,802	506,885	250,957	626,040	0
		7,800	140,065	515,148	278,736	653,819	0
		7,800	148,394	523,477	308,783	683,866	0
		159,000					0
		7,800	156,781	531,864	341,275	716,358	0
		0	111,217	485,360	322,180	669,854	44,163
		0	63,072	436,392	302,888	620,886	44,163
		0	12,203	384,828	283,473	569,322	44,163
		0	0	0	264,030	529,287	44,163
		0	0	0	244,641	496,214	44,163
		0	0	0	225,324	475,580	44,163
		0	0	0	206,167	453,241	44,163
		0	0	0	187,284	429,019	44,163
		0	0	0	168,812	402,721	44,163
		163,800	0	0			397,467
		0	0	0	150,924	374,153	44,163
		0	0	0	133,709	359,060	44,163
		0	0	0	117,343	343,681	44,163
		0	0	0	102,030	328,023	44,163
		0	0	0	87,995	312,090	44,163
		0	0	0	75,475	295,858	44,163
		0			64,625	291,099	44,163
		0			55,721	287,799	44,163
		0			49,110	286,191	44,163
		0			45,140	286,490	44,163

163,800	0	0			839,097
0	0	0	44,197	288,930	44,163
0	0	0	46,947	276,388	44,163
0	0	0	53,952	263,997	44,163
0	0	0	65,862	251,825	44,163
0	0	0	83,482	240,030	44,163
0	0	0	107,791	228,857	44,163
0	0	0	138,732	269,800	44,163
0	0	0	177,035	318,923	44,163
0	0	0	223,451	377,036	44,163
0	0	0	278,768	444,992	44,163
163,800	0	0			1,280,727
0	0	0	343,869	523,744	44,163
0	0	0	419,648	614,260	44,163
0	0	0	507,089	717,601	44,163
0	0	0	607,339	835,001	44,163
0	0	0	721,528	967,681	44,163
0	0	0	850,820	1,116,897	44,163
0	0	0	996,185	1,283,703	44,163
0	0	0	1,158,757	1,469,327	44,163
0	0	0	1,339,843	1,675,183	44,163
0	0	0	1,540,755	1,902,688	44,163
163,800	0	0			1,722,357
0	0	0	1,763,394	2,153,883	44,163
0	0	0	2,018,523	2,355,799	44,163
0	0	0	2,311,111	2,584,437	44,163
0	0	0	2,646,670	2,843,737	44,163
0	0	0	3,032,909	3,139,589	44,163
0	0	0	3,461,955	3,577,437	44,163
0	0	0	3,937,405	4,062,393	44,163
0	0	0	4,463,746	4,598,999	44,163
0	0	0	5,047,727	5,194,088	44,163
0	0	0	5,693,739	5,852,108	44,163
163,800	0	0			2,163,987
0	0	0	6,408,891	6,580,251	44,163

The above illustration gives us a practical example of the benefits of IUL (non-qualified plan) over 401(k)/IRA(qualified plan). Amanda was 30 years old when she found out about a better alternative to prepare towards her retirement. We did not take a penny from her. We used the same money she was already spending. When we met her she was putting $500.00 per month into her 401(k) and 50.00 per month into a whole life policy which gave her a death benefit of $75.000.00.She was also paying $50.00 per month into a cancer policy which was worth $50.000.And $ 50.00 per month was going into a mutual fund account. We took the exact same money into an index universal life and this was the result.

She will make this contributions for only 20 years and she will receive an annual income check for $44,163 tax –free beginning at age 51 all the way to age 100.She does not have to wait no 591/2 year old. Remember I said, the earlier, the better. In our retirement plan you can retire at any age. That annual income can be in hundreds of thousands of dollars all the way to age 100 **tax-free**. You determine how long and how much. She would also have cash value building in the policy which she can cash out as a lump sum or whatever amount she needs in case she lost her job or for other emergencies. Her new death benefit will be $375,083.Therefore she does not need the whole life policy. Her new policy also gives her critical illness coverage up to 90% of her new death benefit for free in case of cancer.

In order for her to pass on generational wealth we set up a trust for her. The IUl will fund the trust. The trust will have clauses which will determine how the money will be disburse to her descendants Church, foundation etc. For example if she was tithing $ 4,500 from her annual income, the church will still receive money from the trust during her retirement and even after her death the church will still receive a lump sum from her death benefit and more money thereafter from all the proceeds from her descendants on the trust. For example, if she dies at age 90and she has a clause in the trust that says 20% to the Church; the Church would receive a lump sum of about $ 416,000. Therefore the church, the descendants and the other organizations she was supporting while she was alive will still receive money from her trust after she is death. And so the tithing will never stop. This will allow her to keep on sponsoring the work of the gospel even in her grave and the church will never worry about money. In most churches right now if a member dies, the tithes stops. But with the trust the tithes never stops. Her descendants, her Church and foundation will receive money into perpetuity.

Business owners: For business owners go to www.globalfd.com and see how you can retire within 10 years with Tax-free money by using OPM (other people's money). This OPM will also be a tax write off to your corporation.

For those who already have life insurance (not Death insurance).

These are some of the things you need to look after in the policy:

a) *Make sure the premium is flexible. This feature will help you not to lose the policy when you are sick or under financial constraints. It will help you to reduce your premium or even skip payments for a while as long s there is enough cash value in the policy.*

b) *Does the policy have living benefits?: This is very important, because when people have critical, chronic or terminal illnesses, they usually can't work. This benefit will kick in to help pay the bills and take care of the family.*

c) *Is your investment in cash value secure, or is it in stock market unsecured?*

d) *Is it term or permanent? Term is rental insurance. No equity.*

e) *What is the interest rate? Remember the rule of 72*

401(k) stories

1) **Mr. Bob:** *I met Mr. Bob in 2009 through his wife. She was in the process of refinancing their house when she met me. When she saw one of our programs on mortgages she was interested and she decided to set up an appointment for me to meet with the husband. Anyway, Bob like most folks wouldn't say much when a product was being presented. He listened carefully and checked me out. But after the presentation he opened up. He told me he has just lost fifteen thousand dollars from his 401(K). And he added that a couple of months ago he wanted to pull out some money, but when he heard about the penalty he decided to leave it alone. But the market got worse and worst until he loss all his money. This might not mean much to some of you but that was all his savings. At the end Bob said, "But the saddest part of it all was that they finally let me go." Proverb 19: 8 states, He who gets wisdom loves his own soul; he who keeps understanding will find good.*

2) **The Kangelo Family:** *This was the case whereby the wife told me her husband will never again mess with 401(K) because of the way they treated him with his own money. She said when her*

husband lost his job; they ran out of money and were financially broke. So the only alternative was for him to pull out some money from his 401(k), but little did he know that it was going to cost him more money on pay back days. He had to pay back the loan with penalties and that made him angry. At the time I met him, he had no investment, so he decided to get on board with a tax –free retirement program.

CHAPTER FIVE

Stumbling Blocks and Barriers to Wealth Building

1) Procrastination: I will do it tomorrow. I don't have time right now. I will be ready next month. Then Monday morning comes, we go to work to pay our bills. Well if you do not take action right now you might remain in the rat race of running around like a chicken without a head paying your bills. That's what the system has been designed for. Then one year passes by. Click you are 30, click you're 40, and click you are 50, and nobody likes the next click. Procrastination is the thief of time.

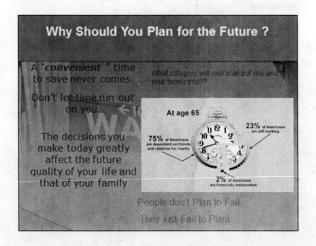

2) The money excuse: I often hear people say I don't have money. They may be genuine to that statement. Wealth creation is not about money is in the structure. I know of someone who will beg for at least $25 from others so he can invest towards his future. That may sound ridiculous, but that is the difference between an employee and an investor, the rich and the poor. Therefore the rich get richer and the poor poorer. A guy who regularly went out to the streets of Washington to beg was able to collect a million dollars and today the rest is history. Please do not be a day dreamer, let your moves force others to dream. Be a pacesetter. Go out of the norm and create your own way to get to the place of milk and honey. The rich use their money challenges as their diving force to a new discovery for others to follow thereby making wealth. Now the middle class use their money challenges to get more J-O-B (just over broke). The poor beg to spend while an investor begs to maintain or increase his financial portfolio. The investor is a long-term ranger. He is futuristic. The thinking of the poor is "eat now" and by so doing, they eat their seeds.

2(i) **Not paying yourself first:** People who often make this statement (the money excuse) have also not learned another secret of the rich, which is paying yourself first. They work to pay everybody, but not themselves. Pay yourself first and everybody last. Tell the credit card companies to hold on. They want to make money out of your hard earned money, by investing your money, and through the high interest rate they place on those cards. Tell them next time to hold on. Pay yourself first by investing. When you pay yourself first it will challenge you to look for other methods and ways to create money to pay your bills and your creditors.

2(ii) **Business owners**: Get your business incorporated so that you can enjoy the tax advantage that has been given to you. It will help you to pay yourself more money. It will give you the opportunity to invest big and still get your money back.We will teach how to use other people's money within 5years and you will not worry about money for the rest of your life.

2(iii) **what's in your refrigerator:** Open it up and you will see money. Most of the things or items in some of our refrigerators are wasted money. Most of those items will end up in trash cans. There are fruit and other items that we buy every week. These have become part of the decorations in our kitchens. They will stay there, go bad, and the next time we are in the store or market, we go for more. Stop complaining saying that you don't have the money. That's the money to invest that you are throwing away. Stop being penny wise and pound foolish. **My advice is** "do not go to market or grocery store when you are hungry." You will end up buying things (in most cases unhealthy things) that you don't need. Do not go to the mall or shopping centers because you feel like it. Be purpose driven. Do not use credit cards for unnecessary leisure. That is not financial intelligence. EMPLOYEES EARN MONEY TO SPEND, WHILE INVESTORS EARN MONEY TO REINVEST TO CREATE MORE MONEY.

THE KEY TO A GREAT INVESTMENT IS FINANCIAL DISCIPLINE. That $15 dollar you are spending foolishly can create you millions in years to come. If you can't discipline yourself, then call Mr. Banker. This is where you need him to help. Commit to him a certain amount for automatic withdrawals from your checking account to your investors. This will help you not to miss your investment contributions, and will prevent mismanagement of your funds.

3) **The fear factor:** God has not given us the spirit of fear (2 Timothy 1:7). Get rid of fear. The only fear you should have should be the fear of God.

Ecclesiastes 12:13 says, "Let us hear the conclusion of the whole matter: Fear God and keep His commandments, for this is man's all." Read also matthew 10:28.

Do not allow fear to shut up the potential in you. If, I might lose, is your current fear, what about the fear of retiring broke and nothing to show forth? Let that fear push you to take charge right now so that you can retire with financial independence. You can't be a winner, a victor, a champion and successful if you are not willing to sacrifice. God had to sacrifice himself in order to win.

The fear factor is also a major difference between the poor and the rich. Rich folks see their challenges as a stepping stone to the next level. They have the risk-taking spirit of an entrepreneur. Like Jacob, be bold and be courageous. Have the never give up spirit, and you will be on your way of becoming a household name to the glory of the Father.

4) **Marital issues**: Some folks will not invest in anything (especially in life investment) due to the beliefs and opinions of their spouse. Husband and wife need to come together and plan for their retirement and their children's college future. It does not matter what your belief system is, some kind of investment has to be done. If not, the reality will catch up with you as you get older.(Read Matthew 12:25).Even if yours is kingdom investment, God is faithful to rewards us here on earth and thereafter. The

Lord wants us to have the abundant life. He does not want us to live like paupers and all over us is written, "broke." That does not glorify Him. Create some investment avenues in order for him to transfer the wealth of the wicked (Mark 10:29-30, John 10;10b, Deuteronomy 8:18, Proverb 13:22, Eccleciastes 6:2.)

5) **Lack of knowledge**: A lot of a people do not know what is happening around them. Listen, learning is continues as long as there are things changing around us. All they do is, go to work, go to work, go to work. Even with the 401(k) or the retirement benefits at their job, they don't know what is happening with it. By the time they retire their lack of knowledge will catch up with them. Get to know what is happening in the economy and with your money. Be informed, be current, so that you will not end up back into the work force. Seek financial advice. Ask questions, educate yourself financially and choose the right investment options.

The Lord wants you to move forward not backward (Hosea 4:6 Exodus 14:15).

6) Instant gratification:

Ecclesiastes 7:4 says, yes, a wise man thinks (much) of death, while the fool thinks only of having a good time now.

Life is for today and tomorrow. We can't live our lives for today's pleasures. Some people prefer to spend long hours at the clubs and bars drinking and partying. They drink away their lives and endanger their lifespan. Tomorrow's enjoyment is not in their agenda. They don't care about who is going to take care of their responsibilities when they die. Little do they know that the kind of activities they are engaged in only soaks away their lives.

They have the mindset that the government is going to take care of them. **Be it the community or the government** there is little to no help nowadays coming from those ends. Today's government is too broke to take care of anybody. It is still struggling to swim out of trillions of debt. Do not allow the pleasures of today to deprive you of tomorrow's preparations. Get your house in order. Lay the foundations for generational wealth. REMEMBER, THE OLDER YOU GET, THE LESSER YOUR STRENGTH. LET MONEY DO ALL THE WORK AT THAT TIME.

AN EVIL UNDER THE SUN/ Other Enemies to Wealth Building

Banks: These guys are not your friends. Be careful how you eat with them. They use our money to make money, and they give us little or nothing in return. They survive on arbitrage. This is the strategy of using other people's money to make more money. They do not keep our money in the vaults. That is why it is good to pull out the equity from the four walls of your house and also invest it at a higher interest rate. Most millionaires understand arbitrage while the average man does not know how money works. Therefore, we do not find a lot of banks in rich neighborhoods. We instead have more banks where middle class folks live. They know that most of these folks do not know how money works. Some do not even know how to manage their money. Therefore they end up paying ridiculous charges for insufficient funds and penalties for overdrafts.

Our checking accounts and saving accounts have no sensible interest rates. Our monies are used to give out loans with high interest rates, and in return we are paid back through credit cards with high interest rates. I am not saying that you should not put money in the bank. It is necessary for liquidity purposes. But you can't make money through bankers.

Taxation: It does not matter how much money you are going to make, if you have to pay taxes on it (especially in the next few years) you might end up having nothing. Projections show that taxes are going to increase due to the high debts. Some are huge like Mount Everest. The more the percentages of the amount we have to pay in taxes, the more money we lose. We recommend you pay taxes on the seed rather than on the harvest. We recommend also tax-free investment vessels such as municipal bonds, Roth IRA, and life insurance. But life insurance is the best. On this topic, see the book TAX-FREE RETIREMENT by Patrick Kelly.

One of the major components to any retirement strategy is taxes. It does not matter whether you are a low income earner or a high income earner. We will show you how tax is your friend and not your enemy and an asset and not a liability. Now let me ask you. What direction do you think tax rates are going to go? If you think anticipated tax rate will be lower, then saving today in a qualified plan makes a lot of sense. But if you think it will be higher, then you want to consider investing in a tax –free environment.

Why They Don't Buy Life Insurance:

1) Stinginess and greediness (two cousins): Imagine the guy who refuses to buy life insurance investment because he believes that when he dies the wife is going to squander the money with other men. The same guy died and the community was forced to raise money for him and his family. Be careful, nobody knows the

time or the hour. This is not wisdom, but foolishness. The bible says, "he that knows what is right and does not do it, to him it is a sin (James4:17). Do the right thing and God will take care of the rest.

Proverb 3:27 says, "do not withhold good from those to whom it is due, when it is in the power of your hand to do so."

2) Background and community: We are a product of our environment. Faith comes by hearing and hearing by the word of God (Romans 10:17). What you keep hearing is very instrumental to either make you or break you. For example," you can't die now". "You are too young to die. It's a waste of money. Girl you've got social security, etc". The truth is, our behavioral patterns were shaped by the people around us, by what they practiced and what they continually said to us. If they did not invest, why must you. If they don't buy life investment, why must you. Nobody has it, so why must I. Our parents did not have it. But that was the 19th century. If you are living in a community, whereby others are blind about this subject, (Matthew 5:14), follow your heart, follow the truth, pursue your goals and follow your convictions.

3) **Ignorance** (the step brother of laziness): some people are naturally too lazy to search out the right information. These kind of people will end up losing 85% of their nest egg to Uncle Sam. The fact that you do not know the existence of something does not mean it does not exist. **Ignorance is not an excuse for failure**.

   a) Un-friendly friends: There are those who claim to be friends inside, but enemies outside. They would not give you the right advice, but when you fall they would laugh at you. There are so many of them in town. Be mindful of the kind of friends you hang out with.

   b) Ignorant friends: They talk about things they do not know as if every finger is equal. They behave as if they know a whole lot. Though some of them are well educated, they are known as educated- ignorant. For colleges do not teach everything you need to know to succeed in this life. Use your conscience, self-discipline and wisdom when they speak out of ignorance.

4) Arrogance: *Proverbs 12:15, A fool thinks he needs no advice, but a wise man listens to others (The Living Bible).*

What can he tell me attitude. I was there before you came. I know it all. We were here when it all started. Jesus also encountered some arrogant folks during His ministry on Earth (John 8:52-58). We must learn to adapt and receive changes. Change is part of life. They had head knowledge in the law, but not revelational knowledge about who Jesus really was. Get rid of arrogance. Don't think you know everything. We have a lot of intelligent but ignorant folks, intelligent but broke folks, intelligent but arrogant folks. They wouldn't go anywhere because they always argue when a new idea challenges the way they think. But a truly intelligent guy will welcome new ideas and do research.

Proverbs 13:10. By pride comes nothing but strife, but with the well-advised is wisdom. Read also Proverbs 25:2.

5) Misunderstanding of God's word:
Proverb 13:22, A good man leaves an inheritance to his children's children, but the wealth of the sinner is stored up for the righteous.

According to this scripture, if one is a good parent they will leave an inheritance to their children or children's children. That means that any parent who will not leave an inheritance is not good. If you do not have it right now, plan to do it when you get back to your feet. Some parents die and all they leave behind is a mountain of debt, through credit cards, mortgage loans, and more loans. Please do not allow the creditors to harass and force your family into modern day slavery, (working to pay unending debts) after you are gone.
See 2kings 4:1.
Life insurance you don't die to use is one of the vessels you can use to leave wealth to your children's children. The wealth of papa Abraham was a generational wealth. It is still flowing till today. That is why the Jews are the richest folks on earth. In his days they left mostly properties, livestock, gold and lands as their own form

of life insurance. But in our days or in the western world not many are privileged to leave this kind of inheritance. But most can leave behind cash through insurance investments. It is biblical. It is the unbelief against it that is not biblical (Proverb 3:27).

CHAPTER SIX

THE EVANGELIST

The Life Insurance That Is Free.

Everlasting life: The other kinds of life insurance I talked about are necessary for us to have. They will help us take care of our immediate, short term and long term liabilities, before and after we leave this world. The precise time we're going to exit this world is not known by any except the Almighty God. There is therefore a need for another kind of insurance. We will need this insurance with us when leaving this world. The good news about this insurance is that there is no premium or monthly charges. All the benefits are free. The death benefit amount is unlimited and the policy is already paid up. Some of you may have heard of it or already have it. The name of the product is called EVERLASTING LIFE.

This life insurance is to protect us from eternal damnation and to secure a place for us in the other world. No insurance carrier has or offers this product even though it is free. The only carrier of this product is J&C de Way Inc. All you need to do is to confess Jesus Christ, the way, as your Lord and Savior and it will be all yours, free. I encourage you to buy index universal life, but Everlasting Life is a must have.

For what will it profit a man if he gains the whole world and losses his soul? Mark 8:36

MINISTERS AND GENERATIONAL WEALTH.

Financial Security:

My experiences and personal encounter with a lot of ministers reveals that most do not have investments set up. Ministers, you need to think about your retirement because most of you right now do not have any. And please do not forget you are in a job whereby there is no job security. What do I mean by that? Anybody can frame a story one day and the church board might kick you out. Some ministers were ex-communicated from their assembly because a lady, or someone, came and told the church the minister impregnated her or slept with her. After the investigations it was too late to restore such men. Their families had to suffer because they had nothing to fall back on. There are others who suffered from breakaways, and other rumors that left them wounded and brokenhearted. Others had to look for miniature jobs because they were not wise enough to have invested for their family and children. The heart of men is desperately wicked (Jeremiah 17:9). Nobody really knows who is who. Some folks are agents. Be wise when it comes to ministerial security.

Financial challenges:

Since most ministers are self-employed, they turn to rely on congregational support and faith for a better tomorrow. Ministers should stop depending on love offerings. **Some ministers are just lazy**. Lack of money has destroyed most ministers' marriages and has caused their children to hate the work of the ministry and disregard the calling in their lives. Some kids have ended up backsliding. Most pastors have no investment avenues. I, therefore, recommend life insurance investment to ministers, because as self-employed, they can independently structure and manage their accounts at their own pace, enjoy the full benefits of a tax-free investment and that of a non-profit organization. Put aside at least 10% of your income into an investment account. The church can take it upon them to pay the premiums.

Most of the mega churches were not built through tithes and offerings. Most of the money came from member's personal investments. I am of the opinion that ministries should invest part of their income into other business ventures, investment avenues, as well as buy shares and create jobs for members instead of trying to give them constant supports and donations. Remember there must be an income before an outcome. You wouldn't survive in the welfare ministry if there is nothing coming in.

Pastors get your people involved. If the people are financially healthy then 75% of the church's challenges will be solved. Ministers your assignment is not only to preach **giving, giving** and **tithing**. You have been preaching it all these years but to no avail, why? It is because they do not know where or how to get more money. **Pastors,** create seminars or meetings where your people can be taught, and where they can be directed to genuine avenues in which they can generate money or more money. **Chop change in envelopes wouldn't cut it**.

I was shocked that statistic shows that **20% of Christians do not pay tithes**. The statistic also shows that it is even worse amongst the Charismatics and Pentecostals. Get wisdom, get understanding. Members hold their pocket the more you hammer on giving because most 21st century believers no longer given by revelation but by sight. This is because they have been duped before by fake ministers. But if you teach your **members** practical ways to make more money, or get professionals to help, their giving will increase. **Get experts to teach your members aspects such as investments, business maintenance, financial discipline, business opportunities** etc. Please, ministers who are already there should not despise those who are still in the days of their small beginnings.

Church builders are investors: I remember when I made this statement at TBN (Trinity Broadcasting Television Network) an elderly lady admitted immediately to one of the guys that she was a living testimony. She is living it. She is at the point in her life whereby she is able to right big checks from her investment accounts without blinking. For Some churches their members will have to work more hours in order to stop the pastor from screaming from Haggai chapter one. Investors do not need to work more hours to build the church because they already have the money in their accounts. But I personally believe folks will be more encouraged to pull out money from products that are tax-free and have no penalties. Some will even go as far as leaving money to the church as their beneficiaries because the joy of the lord's house has consumed them.

Retirement plan:

'This is what pertains to the Levites: From twenty-five years old and above one may enter to perform service in the work of the tabernacle of meeting; vv.25 and at the age of fifty years they must cease performing this work, and shall work no more.(Numbers 8:24-25)

This scripture is a proof that even God believes in retirement. The day I discovered this scripture my eyes popped open. I was shocked. Yes, you will not retire completely from your passion, but God still acknowledges the fact that this mortal body is going to get weaker someday. The question is, "what will you do if there were no retirement structure set up by you or the ministry?" Some of you are almost getting there or, are already there, and you do not have any yet. Yes the Lord is able to supply all our needs, but He made sure the ministry took care of the Levites. That is why you need to wake up. Faith is not foolishness.

A wise man thinks ahead; a fool doesn't, and even brags about it.
Proverbs 13:16 (The Living Bible)

You must not die and leave your seed begging for bread like the prophet in 2 kings 4:1-7. Instead of leaving behind inheritance like the bible says, he left only debt. He was a full time genuine prophet. How can a sound prophet, or minister die and his children be used as collateral for the debt he owed. No wonder a lot of minister's kids are turning away from the faith. But that will not be your portion because today you have been delivered. Please do not destroy the good moral foundation you have labored for, for years for your seeds because of a little mistake. Do not die and leave your family to the point whereby they can't even afford to give you a decent burial. Make sure you invest or do something for yourself while in ministry so that when you physically retire, you will not be looking unhappy, because of no money. At least get some life insurance investments.

Ecclesiastes 6:3-5 Even if a man has a hundred sons and as many daughters and lives to be very old, but leaves so little money at his death that his children can't even give him a decent burial—I say that he would be better off born dead. For though his birth would then be futile and ends in darkness, without even a name, never seeing the sun or even knowing its existence, yet that is better than to be an old, unhappy man (The Living Bible).

The Misery, The Dilemma of Financial Crisis:

Monetary challenges have landed so many ministers into arenas and into issues that are embarrassing and disgraceful to the body of Christ. The main reason is because they were solely depending on love offerings to sustain them in ministry; and when they don't have enough, they grip, force, and use all kinds of spiritual gimmicks to pull out money from folks. Some ministers have smuggled believer's salaries away in the name of Jesus giving them some kind of miracle. However, there are still faithful ministers out there trying to raise money for kingdom agendas. But, if you are in ministry in order to make money, you will be disappointed and you will fail. If that is you, you need to repent and the Lord will show you a genuine way to become wealthy.

Word of Wisdom: Do not break a potential relationship because an individual did not give you a particular amount of love offering you expected. Money must not take precedence over relationship. To be relationally poor is the worst poverty.

Solutions and Strategies to Help Churches and Members toward Financial Independence:

Strategy#1 set up a tax-free investment account for your organization.

71

Strategy #2 you will be taught how to set up a trust fund and a foundation. A trust fund and a foundation will be set up.

Strategy #3 Thrive to build generational wealth.

Strategy#4 You will be shown how to invest the right way without using big money.

Strategy#5 Multiplying member's income and decreasing outcome

Strategy#6 Setting up a tax-free college accounts for the children.

Strategy #7 How to turn your home equity from being Mr. Banker's money to your money so that you will always have liquid cash.

Strategy #8 How to knock the strongman of mortgage. **Mortgage** *is from a French word, mort, which means death. It will help you to come out of this death and be the real owner of your properties.*

Strategy #9 Helping business owners to get free money to invest.

Strategy #10 Church financing and wealth transfer to the church.

Remember these nuggets:

Anointing without money is annoyance. Money amplifies the anointing. Money gives the anointing an expression. It advertises the anointing.

If you are not in the know, you are not in the flow. Get yourself updated and remain relevant. What you do not understanding, do not criticize.

The anointing you do not respect, will not bless you.

Whatever you fight against, you can't experience. If you do not have the right attitude towards those whom the Lord has blessed, then you can't be blessed, because you are abusing the favor of God upon their lives by your attitude. The Lord told Abraham He would bless those who bless him and curse those who curse him (Genesis

12:2-3). Do not judge someone else's servant. The Lord himself is the discipline master.

CHAPTER SEVEN

WHERE DO I GO FROM HERE?
WHAT DO I DO NOW?

I n this case you will have to become **the searcher** and **the doer**. The searcher does the findings and the doer puts the findings into action.

The Searcher:
   A) Your future
      1) **Find out God's plan for your life**: Ask him why he created you. What is his purpose for your life? He did not send you here for you to live a routine-labor life. You were not made just to wake up in the morning, brush your mouth, wash your face, catch the bus, go to work, eat launch, come back home, eat supper, watch some TV, go to bed, wake up again and start all over. Then one day you ultimately die and you leave the world. God did not call us into a routine way of life. You have to seek out your mission on earth from him. You have to find out whose or which problem you were born to solve. I assure you that if you seek him you will find him. He will show you great and mighty things. He will reveal to you hidden treasures.(Isaiah 55:6,Jeremiah 33:3)

2) **Find out where your passion is**: It is an indicator of who you were born to be. It is the conductor leading you to your destiny. Passion is that thing which you can do 24/7 without boredom.

3) **Gift and talent diagnosis**: What is it that you can easily learn? What can you do without struggling? What are you good at? Look for your strength. But it must not be illegal, sinful or crime driven. If it does, then it is obsolete.

4) **The problem and solution test**: Whose problem can you solve? Whose problem do you have the solution for? Joseph was able to solve the Egyptian's problem and that made him the governor.

5) **Protégée and mentor search**: Search for those who can connect you or help you to your land of milk and honey. We call them destiny helpers or divine connectors. They may be someone who has the right info, right knowledge. It may be someone who has been there before (been there, done that), or knows someone who has or need what you have. The mentor will derive satisfaction as the protégée gets fulfillment.

B) Your finance

1) **Spenders**: Find out if you are a big spender. Are you a window shopper? Where do you spend most of your money? What do you buy the most? Are you stealing from God's money while spending (God's armed robbers)**?** You can't enter into the wealth zone if you don't know where your money is going. You need to track it down so that you can have plenty of seed to sow. Plenty of seed will speed up wealth accumulation which will lead you faster into your wealth zone.

2) **Storehouses**: Where is your money? Is it in the banks or stock market? Who takes care of your storehouses? Is it you, the bankers or the stockbrokers? Who is your financial advisor? Does he or she know how money works? Do not allow others to gamble with your life. You need to find answers to some of these questions.

3) **Debts**: MR creditor wants you to stay in debts. Find out how much you owe him and get rid of those huge and never ending balances.

4) **Taxation**: Find out your tax bracket and your money. Find out if your money is classified as tax-now, tax-later, or tax-never.

5) **Insurance**: What kind do you have? Dead or living, permanent with equity(cash back) or rental with zero returns? Do your research. It is the glory of kings to search out a matter.(proverbs 25:2)

The Doer (after the search is over, he puts the findings into action and action brings output, results)

A) Your Future

1) **Business partnership**: Partner with a business owner who already has a clientele base in order for you to grow quicker.

2) **Creditors**: Use their money when it has zero interest rate attached. A brother did just that. He took the creditors money with zero interest rate for one year as his capital, to start his car business. He turned the money around within one year and paid his creditors back their money with no extra. He now continues the business with the profit. Today money is not his problem.

3) **Global business**: strive to start a business, create or invent a product that will satisfy everybody (believers and unbelievers). For example, do not put a business name that will turn certain folks away. Penetrate the different cultures around you. Have a cultural mind shift.

4) **Sales**: Start selling something. It might be small. But don't look down on yourself. Selling is the way up. It is the way to financial independence. You can create your own system or follow an existing system whereby you determine how much you make. No selling equals no profit which equals no money. I pity those who look down on selling. It is because they do not know that this

is the secret. Show me a man who has made it big time and you will find a man who was able to sell something. The difference between the poor and the rich is that, the poor are afraid to market themselves and their values, while the rich do the exact opposite. More on this in our seminars. SELLING GIVES YOU THE REVELATION TO MAKE MONEY.

5) **Network marketing**: Some of you may have to join a network marketing company whose product you believe in, and you have a passion for it. The road to the top might be very rugged, but persevere and the rest will be history. You might not enter your wealthy place immediately but you will learn how to run a profitable business. You will acquire skills in administration, marketing, public speaking, customer relations, telephone ethics, sales and much more. And these skills will be tremendously vital in ministry. My exposure into network marketing (and with the Lord on my side) was the catalyst to a billion dollar idea for a billion dollar soul mind set in my life. More on this in our seminars. Learn how to recruit help.

6) **Do not wait for opportunities to come to you. Create** them. How? **Market yourself. Learn to take care of yourself first, before the credit card companies.**

B) FINANCES:

1) **Pay yourself first**: Most of us work for money only to end up paying our mortgages, rents, cars, utilities bills, credit cards, club membership fees, and anything or anybody we signed a contract to pay every month. But you, who work for that money regardless of rain or sun, with sickness or tiredness, end up with nothing in your account. This has got to stop. One of the ways to pay yourself, is to commit a certain amount to an investment that will yield dividends. Do it on a regular basis. It does not matter how small the amount is. Make sure you take

care of your future before you pay the creditors. If you do not know how to do this yourself, ask your bank to automatically deduct a certain amount from your income on a regular basis. Please, do this as soon as possible. Do not procrastinate.

1) **Do a Financial analysis**: To know exactly how much you can pay yourself every month, you will need to know how much is coming in and how much is going out (income # outcome).

2) **Stop unnecessary shopping and spending**: (Proverbs 21:20) There is still a tomorrow for you to live into. No money, no honey. Take your time and plan for it. Do not be in a rush or compete. Remember, no body plans to fail, but no planning is preparation to failure.

3) **Pay your tithes**: Investing by stealing God's money won't work. Financial devourers in the market will wipe your money out. It is not a good idea to steal from God in order to invest (Haggai 1:9-10).

4) **Giving**: It is the secret to increase your financial portfolio. When you give, you receive more seed to invest. And the more the seed, the bigger the harvest.

Luke 6:38 says "Give and it will be given to you: good measure, pressed down, shaken together, and running over will be put into your bosom. For with the same measure that you use, it will be measured back to you."

5) **Open an investment account**: We recommend a tax-free account. There are some of them in this book. After you have done step one to five, decide on how much you want to start with. It does not matter the amount. **Start right away. Timing** plays a very vital role in **investment.** The more you wait to have much more money the lesser your opportunity to benefit from rule 72.

HOW TO ENTER THE WEALTH ZONE

No one can enter the wealth zone if they are afraid of risks or failure. But you don't have to enter into a casket or perform some kind of satanic rituals. That is not God's way to enter. The wealth zone of God is open to all of God's children who do not compromise HIS standard. Resist the spirit or the voice that says you will fail. Get rid of that thought. Give it a deaf ear and ride on. Make up your mind to learn from your mistakes. Failure is not an enemy to success, but it is an eye opener to the real problem or where the need is. Have the "never give up" kind of mentality. What you need to do is to get uncomfortable in your comfort zone and make up your mind to come out of it. **Do not belittle yourself**. For what you see is what you get. The question is, what do you see? You must strive to increase your capacity. Aspire to create and be unsatisfied where you are. Do not get distracted. Stay focused to the plan and to the vision. Be determined to fight and resist oppositions. Learn financial discipline and stay humble. Do **not wait for money**. If you do, money will never come. It will never be enough. Start walking, working, and moving. Money will catch up with you. Step out by faith and the lord will send help. Market yourself to individuals you know will need your goods and services, gifts or talent. You've got to be sick and tired of living from only one source of income. Long for multiples, or unending sources of income. Have activities to do every day that will take you to your vision. Do not wish desire or dream to be rich. But commit to be rich. What are you doing? **Do something**.

THE BEST FINANCIAL INDEPENDENCE IS RESIDUAL INCOME. THAT IS, MONEY COMING TO YOU, EVEN WHEN YOU ARE NOT WORKING. Do the work or business once and earn money for it again and again.

WHAT YOU NEED TO KNOW

You need to know that when God wants to bless you, time and space will not be any barrier. You need to know that you don't have to play the waiting game.

You need to know that opportunities come and go. When you see one, grab it. But it must not contradict Godliness. You need to know that opportunities are everywhere. The question is, what do you see? Do you have a vision?

You need to know you must not only be a dreamer but a creator. You have the Elohimistic characteristics of the Almighty in you.

You need to know that you will not reap if you do not sow. Sowing and reaping is the principle that keeps men focusing. Men spend all their lives in something they believe because they know they will reap. Athletes spend their lives practicing in order to win a prize. A lady spends one year in a boot camp with no contact to the world in order to become an Olympic champion. Know the season in which you are.

You need to know that if you are an employee and your company is your only source of income, you can't be richer than your employer. The Lord will need to bless the employer first before he (the employer) can give you raises or bonuses. And you need to know in some cases that even after all your prayers **you are paid back by getting fired.** t

You need to know how to catch the fish yourself. Work to learn and not to earn. Learn and carry the skills from your job and start yours. Learn from the story of Jacob and Laban.

You need to know that success is connected to action. There is nothing like failure. Failure is a step on the ladder of the learning curve. The challenge you are facing is a promotion. It is not meant to kill you. There is a blessing coming your way.

The ALPHA and OMEGA
(The beginning and the End)

Every Christian investor needs to know that, the secret to your wealthy place is to follow divine leadership. When I talk of divine leadership, I mean going back to the **manufacturer, the Lord Almighty**. He knows the fish that has swallowed your wealth. He knows who has what it takes for you to enter your wealth zone (**P**salms 24:1-21). It does not matter how hard we work, we need to ask him what is that good plan and future that he has for us.

Life becomes very easy when we seek Him diligently for his will, purpose and directions in every life undertaking. After reading this book, go back to the Lord and ask him what to do.

Jeremiah 29:11 For I know the thoughts that I think towards you, says the lord, thoughts of peace and not of evil, to give you a future and a hope

Now I will like you to also know that He is always ready to show you what to do, because it is His will for us to prosper. But with all that prosperity, without Jesus as our personal Lord and Savior, it is useless. He wants us to be rich, but He does not want us to be rich and go to hell. He loves us so much that He wants to bless us here on earth and thereafter take us to heaven. No amount of wealth without Jesus as Savior will be able to give us eternal life. The best thing to do right now before all these principles become really effective and successful in our lives is to surrender to the Lord Jesus. Ask Him to come into your life by forgiving all your sins and accept Him as your Lord and Savior.

It is at this moment you now become a Christian investor. All your labor will not be in vain. He will back you up in your investment procedures and wealth building system. Make sure you tell a Christian friend or a minister the step you just took. Find a bible believing church. Now you can ask the Lord for a billion dollar idea and for a billion dollar souls. You have just received the power to overtake. He will now show you how to enter into your wealth zone (Proverbs 3:5, Psalm 37:7). Accepting HIM is the first and main foundation into the wealth zone for every Christian investor. He knows you best. He knows your strengths and weaknesses. Money is good. To be wealthy is awesome. That is why I am sharing this information in this book with a lot of folks. But wealth without Jesus is the worst error a man can ever make. Please pray this prayer with me.

Lord I know that I am a sinner. I know that if I die right now I am going straight to hell. Lord I also know that if I ask for forgiveness I will be forgiven. Father I am sorry for all my sins, and I ask for your mercy and salvation into my life, in Jesus name today, Amen.

CONFESSIONS to the WEALTH ZONE:

Life and death is in the power of your tongue. Call those things which are not as though there are. Your confession is one of your secret weapons to your wealth zone. The "who" you see, is the "who" you become. Learn to speak to yourself the positives before the enemy speaks the negatives. Make these confessions and other wealth confessions every day. So, let's begin. Say it out loud.

I am a child of God, and because I am created in his image and my Daddy is the creator, I refuse to live a broke life. I am a wealth creator minister. **I'm a kingdom financier.** I've got what it takes to become a global champion and a financial bulldozer. The universe will say yes to me.

I will not die with my gifts. I will release them to make a positive impact in my world. I have the power to make wealth. I have what it takes to excel in life.

I am a lender and not a borrower. I am a wealth distributor. I will lend to nations and nations will borrow from me. I am "unkillable", unshakeable, and **I can't die**. I am money loaded. I am a wealthy, wealthy billion dollar figure. I am a money magnet, a money reservoir and a kingdom builder. My hands are blessed. And everything I touch will be blessed. Money I am your master. Therefore obey me now. I command you to fill up all my store houses, barns, accounts and investment portfolios. I will never be a financial loser. Money is on its way heading towards my direction. I declare that I am a wealthy, wealthy, billion dollar kingdom builder in Jesus' **Name, Amen**.

Wisdom keys: I was told in order for me to be rich I should use:
OPM(other people's money)
OPT(other people's time)
OPI(other people's idea)
OPE(other people's effort)
And there is nothing like LUCK. For L=labor U=understanding C=commitment K=knowledge.

WEALTH AND INVESTMENT CAUTIONS

1) Do not rob God to pay Caesar: Make sure you are a tither, and that you are faithful with your money. If not, your investment will not be fruitful.
2) Do not forget or abandon the God of prosperity in the days of your wealth (Deut 8:18). If you do, it will only cause you more pain and less enjoyment.
3) Stay and remain humble. Do not brag or hit your chest. Remember it was God who took you there.
4) Stay **holy. Godliness** brings gain. Stay away from corrupt minds (1Timothy 6:5-7)
5) Saving accounts are not for investment purposes. They are there to take care of emergencies, such as car problems, housing repairs, etc. Is a Storage account for delayed spending.

OTHER FACTS THAT YOU NEED TO KNOW

Employer's Life Insurance: It is an employee benefit. The day you move from that job it does not go with you. It does not pay you any dividends or cash value. It does not have living benefits. This is not the kind of life insurance we recommend for Christian investors. The insurer has the discretion to increase the premium when you retire. Keep the insurance policy at your job, but get an independent contract whereby you can invest under-tax-free. Do not depend solely on your 401(k) or any tax deferred investment accounts because, as taxes go up so does your tax bracket. It might move from 10%, 15%, and 20% to 40 % and above depending on your class. The bulk of the trillions of debt in the country, which is high like Mount Everest, will definitely be paid by tax payers.

Key Employee Insurance: This insurance is to protect a business from the loss of profits or revenue because of the death of one of its key employees, such as the owner or an executive officer. Any type of individual insurance may be used for this purpose. The business owner is the policy owner, premium payer and the beneficiary.

Health Insurance versus Life Insurance: At least most Christian investors know that, when God created us we were perfectly healthy. Sicknesses and diseases entered this world as a result of sin through

Adam and Eve. When a man is fully born again and receives great revelations from the word of God he can live the rest of his life without health insurance. Life insurance is necessary because it is one of the ways you will leave an inheritance to your family when you go to heaven. It is good that you will be going to heaven, but your family still has a life to live after your departure. While the angels will be rejoicing, your family must not be lamenting. They also need to rejoice with the angels for a saint who has gone home because of the inheritance left behind. After mourning what next?

Auto Insurance: It is good. Most of us have it because we don't want to fall into the hand of the police without it. But nobody wakes up in the morning and pray "Oh God let me have an accident today." We have it for "just in case." The auto insurer will never give us part of the profit he makes with our premiums, even if we are the best driver in town. If you believe in car insurance you should as well believe in life insurance. The poor buy car insurance and stop there, while the rich go a step further to buy investment insurance. They understand and know the secret of profit sharing. Do not live your life to pay others (liabilities). Pay yourself, also. Some of my folks wish the auto insurer would send them some money back after many years of having no accidents; but that is not going to happen.

Working Smart and Retiring Early: When people have enough nest eggs they retire early. People retire from jobs but they do not retire from life. Do not work hard, work smart. It is not how hard you work. You still have a life to live after you retire. One way to work smart is to invest while you are young. You don't want to cruise around with your dream car and a walker (walking stick or cane). You don't want to be zealous to do the Lord's work when you are physically worn out. Another way to work smart is to continually search for knowledge where ever you are and strive to gather the right information about things you want to know. RETIREMENT SHOULD BE ENJOYED NOT ENDURED. In our retirement plan you can retired at any age. You don't have to wait no 591/2 or 65 and above. People have been programmed to think that way and thereby remain slaves to the system.

Profitable versus Unprofitable Debts: Unprofitable debts are those which become a liability or leave you with a heavy financial burden. Such debts include, home mortgages,(for those folks who do not know how to turn it into an asset) car loans, unending credit cards payments, hospital bills and anything that saps money from you without a profitable return. Profitable debts are those you can use to get back a profitable return. Any debt you can use to make you more money or add value to your life is profitable. An example is found in 2kings 4:1-6. The lady in this story did the borrowing that added value to her life. She was able to pay off her debts and live on the profit. So as a Christian investor, you need to know the kind of debts that will help accomplish your dream.

Sole-Proprietors: You can use free money to get tax-free returns, but in order to get it, you need to get your business incorporated. This will allow you to enjoy the benefits of key employee insurance, premium financing, section 79 and much more. Most of you are leaving a lot of money on the table. With premium financing you can retire with tax-free money within 10 years. Go to www.globalfd.com.

College Graduates: Do not get too excited and start buying stuff that you might not be able to pay for in case you lose your job. Learn to start investing money that can help in a six months period even after a job lay off. You can earn a seven figure income and still retire broke if you do not make good choices with your money. My recommendation is to invest. Send the money to work. Start a business.

Do Not Raise Your Life Style Just Because You Have A Raise. Remember your money might be swallowed up as a result of unforeseen circumstances, but your bills which you have increased, will not.

Emigration of Baby Boomers: Due to the financial crisis ahead, most baby boomers are leaving the United States. There are many reasons why most Americans migrate. But the present economic situation and future financial crisis is forcing so many to make other parts of the world their permanent retirement home. Most of these boomers are moving to African countries (e.g. Ghana), European nations (France, Croatia, Italy) South America (Mexico) and some part of Asia. When asked why, most of them said the cost of living in the United States is outrageously high. They prefer to sell all their properties, gather all the pennies, and resettle abroad. This is proof to some of us, that the issues of debt, taxation, inflation and other aspects that this book talked about, is already in existence. The question now is, how is the government going to solve these problems? They might increase taxes. That is not good news either for all tax-deferred investments. Without divine intervention, some people will retire to endure instead of to enjoy. They will retire mourning instead of celebrating. This will not be your portion. We serve a God who reveals hidden secrets.

The message of the Christian investor was supported by the following businesses and organizations:

1) **Jericho Walk Inc.(help you live a healthy lifestyle)**
   11902 Jones Rd Suit # P
   Houston TX 77090
   Phone #+ 832 912 7400

2) **Zion covenant Ministries (prayer and Miracles)**
   Services: seven days a week.
   2340 Barker Oaks Dr.
   Houston TX 77077
   Phone # +281 575 7700

3) **Maischa Bakery (For all your party needs)**
   Molyko –Buea Cameroon
   Phone # +23795259315

4) **Dafyik Financial Services(Accounting Firm)**
   9898 Bissonnet St # 375 D
   Houston TX 77036
   Phone# +713 776 2266

5) **Etabang Enterprises, Inc.(Tax-Free financial services)**
   6495 New Hampshire Ave,#111
   Hyattsville, MD 20783
   Phone #+240 353 8449

6) **Care Dynamics(Home Care Services)**
   3902 Silver Ridge Blvd
   Missouri City TX 77459
   Phone # 713 858 1562

7) **Able Healthcare Solutions, LLC(mentally Challenged Kids)**
   14810 Rancho Vista Dr.
   Houston TX 77083
   Phone# 713 505 6636

8) **Mountain of Prayer and Praise international Ministries**
   8739 Boone Rd Suite D
   Houston, TX 77493
   Phone # 281 748 5018

9) **Houston Praise Center**
   14829 Bellaire Blvd # 12
   Houston TX 77083
   Phone # 713 480 2778

10) **Rehab Network (Nursing Agency)**
    9896 Bissonnet # 345
    Houston TX 77036
    Phone #713 677 0944

11) **The Christian Attorney**
    3806 Live Oaks
    Houston TX 77004
    Phone # 281 501 9295

12) **Shields Capital Group (teaching you generational wealth)**
5757 Ranchester dr. # 100
Houston TX 77036
Phone # 510 967 6525

13) **Oxford Realty(Selling all kinds of Houses)**
Phone: 281 515 2060
Fax: 281 983 0383

14) **The Insurmountable Film works Inc. (A Christian film producing company)**
Producer of the bestselling movie "THE LAND"
Contacts: 713 576 9026, 832 486 0294, 832 890 8620

Reference Materials

Tax-free Retirement by Patrick Kelly

2007

Money cometh to the body of Christ
By Rev(Dr)Leroy Thompson Sr

Harrison House -Tulsa 1999

The Biblical Road to Blessings by pastor Benny Hinns

Thomas Nelson Publishers-Nashville 1997

Sermons by Pastor Emmanuel Olumide
(aka the Apostle of Wisdom)

Ministers Conference 2007 –Turning Point
@CBC Idimo –Lagos Nigeria

Additional Sources to Visit:

www.nationallife.com

www.shieldscapitalgroup.net

www.aca.com

www.irs.gov/retirement

www.ssa.gov/retirment

www.globalfd.com

www.legalzoom.com

For 'The Christian Investor 'wealth creation seminars and conferences for your Church, Organization, Schools and Institutions contact us at:

Zion Covenant Ministries
2340 Barker Oaks, Houston, TX 77077,USA
Phone Numbers: (001)281 575 7700 or (001) 713 576 9026
Fax: 281 575 1822
Emails: pros4jesus@yahoo.com
info@zionbreadoflife.org
Website:www.zionbreadoflife.org

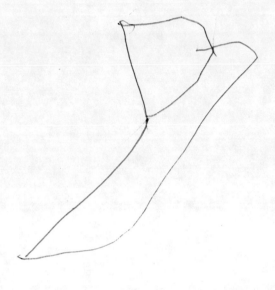

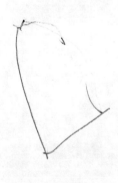

CPSIA information can be obtained at www.ICGtesting.com
Printed in the USA
LVOW082124181011

250895LV00002BA/1/P